Wiccan Kitchen

A GUIDE TO MAGICAL COOKING & RECIPES

LISA CHAMBERLAIN

WITH RECIPE DEVELOPER
Wesley Martin

STERLING ETHOS
New York

STERLING ETHOS
New York

An Imprint of Sterling Publishing Co., Inc.

STERLING ETHOS and the distinctive Sterling Ethos logo are
registered trademarks of Sterling Publishing Co., Inc.

Originally published as *Wicca Kitchen Witchery* in 2017 by Wicca Shorts

This publication is intended for informational purposes only. This publication includes alternative
therapies that have not been scientifically tested. The publisher does not claim that this publication shall
provide or guarantee any benefits, healing, cure, or any results in any respect. This publication is not intended
to provide or replace conventional medical advice, treatment, or diagnosis or be a substitute to consulting with
a physician or other licensed medical or health-care providers. The publisher shall not be liable or responsible
in any respect for any use or application of any content contained in this publication or any adverse effects,
consequence, loss, or damage of any type resulting or arising from, directly or indirectly, the use or application
of any content contained in this publication. Any trademarks are the property of their respective owners,
are used for editorial purposes only, and the publisher makes no claim of ownership and shall
acquire no right, title, or interest in such trademarks by virtue of this publication.

ISBN 978-1-4549-3470-7

Distributed in Canada by Sterling Publishing Co., Inc.
c/o Canadian Manda Group, 664 Annette Street
Toronto, Ontario, Canada M6S 2C8
Distributed in the United Kingdom by GMC Distribution Services
Castle Place, 166 High Street, Lewes, East Sussex, England BN7 1XU
Distributed in Australia by NewSouth Books
University of New South Wales, Sydney, NSW 2052, Australia

For information about custom editions, special sales, and premium and corporate purchases,
please contact Sterling Special Sales at specialsales@sterlingpublishing.com.

Manufactured in China

6 8 10 9 7 5

sterlingpublishing.com

Interior design by Sharon Jacobs
Cover design by Elizabeth Mihaltse Lindy

Picture credits – *see page 210*

For the farmers, the gardeners,
and everyone else who makes the
magic of food possible.

—*Lisa Chamberlain*

Contents

Part Four

EDIBLE MAGIC

---◇---

Introduction

I MAGINE, IF YOU WILL, AN OLD-FASHIONED RURAL cottage in the age before electricity. Candles light the cozy main room, where a woman tends a boiling cauldron over an open fire in the hearth. Jars of flour, sugar, and other dry goods line the rustic wooden shelves above an oak-topped table, upon which several clay bowls filled with herbs are lined up to be ceremoniously emptied into the cauldron.

The brew may be a nourishing soup or stew, a healing medicine, or a potion designed to bring about a specific magical outcome—or a combination of the three. Since all food originates within the sacred bounty of Mother Earth, anything that's edible has inherent magical potential, and the woman at the hearth knows this well.

In myths and folklore from virtually every culture around the world, food has been associated with magic, and some of these ancient traditions have survived into the twenty-first century. Probably the most well-known example is the blowing out of candles on a birthday cake.

It is believed that the first cakes with candles date back to ancient Greece, where they were given as offerings to Artemis, the Greek goddess of the hunt and of the Moon. The cakes were moon-shaped and lit with candles in order to make them "shine" as the Moon does. Eventually, cake came to be used to celebrate birthdays. The practice of birthday candles likely began in eighteenth-century Germany, where it became customary to number the candles on the cake according to the age of the celebrant, with an extra candle added to ensure another full year of life ahead.

These days, with people's life expectancy considerably improved, the "birthday wish" one makes before blowing out the candles could be for anything, but this wish is usually kept secret. And though it may seem to most people simply a fun tradition, there's a kind of dramatic quality to this moment at a birthday gathering that suggests there's more belief in the power of wishing on a candle than the average person might admit.

The wishbone is another tradition with ancient roots, going back to the Etruscans, who used the breastbone of a goose to divine the weather. They would also rub the bone while making a wish. The Romans adapted this custom, using chickens, but due to its popularity, there often weren't enough "wishbones" to go around. Thus, the tradition of two people wishing on the same bone came into being. The bone would be snapped in two, and the holder of the longer piece would see their wish come true.

Another modern custom, the Halloween game of bobbing for apples, is also said to have come from the Romans, who brought cultivated apples with them to the British Isles. As Roman culture merged with that of the Celts, apples came to feature in the Celtic festival of Samhain. The game was played by young single people, and the first to successfully bite into an apple was said to be the next to marry.

Although these few examples of ancient traditions have survived through the millennia, it's fair to say that for the most part, mainstream culture is more disconnected from the magic of food than it has ever been. This is because we are more separated from the sources of our food than *we* have ever been.

For the majority of human history, our ancestors spent much of their waking time actively hunting, growing, and harvesting their sustenance, and therefore appreciating the role played by the Earth, the Sun, the Moon, and the Elements in the process.

These days, we can pull a packaged meal from the freezer, toss it in the microwave, press a few buttons, and have dinner on the table within minutes. Of course, there's a lot to be said for convenience on busy days, but what we gain in time saved is no comparison to what we lose in terms of nutrition, taste, and magical connection to the Earth and all she offers us.

Fortunately, there seems to be a resurgence of interest in many parts of the modern world in returning to a more direct connection to Nature when it comes to food—at least to some extent.

More and more people are growing some of their own herbs and vegetables themselves on family farms, in backyard gardens, and even on windowsills in urban environments. Organic food has become more popular and more accessible over the past few decades, as people wake up to the damage caused by industrialized agriculture to the planet and to our health. At the same time, there has been an increasing interest in the more esoteric aspects of food and food production, leading many to discover the ancient practice now known as "kitchen witchery."

Also known as "kitchen magic," "pantry magic," "culinary wizardry," and other names, the art of intertwining food and magic is a natural pursuit for Wiccans, Witches, and other Pagans who have an affinity for cooking. But the realm of kitchen witchery is also inhabited by people who don't practice magic in any other context, and who may not even consider themselves to be Witches or Pagans of any stripe.

These cooks simply work with an attitude of reverence for the Earth, intuiting the transformative energies of foods and using what they have to create nourishing, magically powerful meals. They may also make medicines, teas, tinctures, candles, and other kitchen crafts that all fall under the umbrella term of "kitchen witchery."

This guide is designed for anyone who is interested in the magical potential of the seemingly ordinary work of preparing and cooking food. While written largely from a Wiccan perspective, most of the information within these pages is simply practical information, useful for anyone from any spiritual background—and any level of cooking ability—who would like to incorporate magical practices into their approach to eating.

Part One delves into the concept of kitchen witchery in the context of our ancient ancestors' relationship to food and our modern esoteric understanding of the magical energies of the Earth's edible abundance. Part Two provides guidance for transforming your kitchen into a sacred space and offers examples of how you can approach the "mundane" act of cooking with a magical eye. Part Three is a mini-grimoire of sorts, with rituals, techniques, tables of correspondences, and an example recipe for making the most out of the magical potential that various foods provide. And in Part Four you'll find magical recipes to help you manifest health, success, and more, as well as seasonal menus for eating in rhythm with the Wheel of the Year.

You don't have to be a master chef or a master magician to find useful information throughout these pages, but even if you are, this guide can still provide new ideas and fresh perspectives on the art of kitchen witchery. So roll up your sleeves and enjoy making magic in your kitchen!

Blessed Be.

Part One

WHAT IS KITCHEN WITCHERY?

THE ANCIENT HEARTH

IT COULD BE ARGUED THAT THE DISCOVERY OF FIRE was the beginning of full-fledged magical practice for our earliest ancestors. Not only did fire allow people to navigate the darkness of night and warm their modest dwellings in the cold months, but it also made it possible to transform previously inedible things like plant roots, stems, certain seeds, and many animal parts into safe, digestible food.

This newfound ability surely must have seemed like a magical blessing from the unseen realms. In fact, the well-known Greek story of Prometheus, the god who took a liking to human beings and decided to bring them the gift of fire, is just one of many ancient myths regarding fire's divine origins.

Of course, to early humans, magic existed everywhere in the prehistoric world, in every aspect of Nature—in the spirits of the land and water, in the cycles of the Moon, in cloud formations and weather patterns, and in the behavior of animals. Plants would almost certainly have had magical significance, as they were one of the primary sources of food, of medicine and, eventually, of shelter for these very early cultures. Indeed, the first "spell" ingredients would have been from plant sources for medicinal remedies. That some plants can kill while others are sources of nourishment and healing was considered a testament to their formidable inherent power.

Yet fire also had a dual nature, one that was arguably more forceful. Able to cause rapid and widespread death and destruction, yet also enhance and sustain life, fire was the first medium through which plants, animals, trees, and even water could be completely transformed, for better or worse, right in front of one's eyes.

The fire over which food was cooked was therefore a very magical thing indeed. And as humans continued to evolve—discovering new food sources, developing new tools for cooking, and adapting their dwellings to accommodate indoor fire—this sacred place eventually became the hearth. It was the focal point of the home, where families gathered to warm themselves, dry wet clothes, bake bread, and cook meals.

As the central, sustaining element of daily life, the fire in the hearth was a living, breathing entity, governed by the deities of the hearth and treated with reverence and respect. This fire was a crucial part of the continuing evolution of what we now call "kitchen witchery."

Obviously, the hearth was not the only context for food-related spiritual practice. Rituals and magical beliefs accompanied every aspect of the acquisition and preparation of food. Ceremonies and offerings honored the deities of hunting and gathering, prayers were sent up for favorable weather and bountiful harvests, and gratitude was expressed to the animals and plants whose lives were taken in order for the people to live. Food was blessed before being consumed, both to offer thanks to the deities who ruled its provenance and to ask for protection from illness. This last practice has continued into modern times, in virtually all religions around the world.

The Earth, Sun, and Moon were revered by the ancients for their roles in the cycles of life and death experienced by all living things, as were the countless solar, lunar, and terrestrial deities associated with abundance and sustenance. Actual food itself was also associated with the divine, as can be seen in the multitude of connections between gods and goddesses and specific foods.

For example, the Celtic god Lugh was associated with both the Sun and the wheat harvest. In ancient Greece, pomegranates were associated with several deities, including Persephone, Zeus, and Dionysus. Foods connected to specific deities would be left out as offerings, as an act of gratitude as well as a prayer for such blessings to continue.

As ancient civilizations evolved, these traditions took root and were passed down from generation to generation, and traces of some of these practices are still present today. Many people throughout Europe still celebrate some version of the four Pagan festivals that marked the turning points of the agricultural year. The most well-known are those of the ancient Celts—Imbolc, Beltane, Lughnasadh, and Samhain—but these holidays go by other names in other parts of Europe, such as Feast of Torches, May Day, Harvest Home, and Winter Nights.

Related to planting, harvesting, and animal husbandry, these festivals were all about the celebration of food in one way or another, with rituals, magic, and feasting as the focal points of the holiday. These special days, along with the ancient solar festivals at the solstices and equinoxes, were later integrated into the Wheel of the Year as followed by Wiccans and many other contemporary Pagans.

In short, it's hard to see how contemporary magical practices could have existed without these ancient food-centered traditions leading the way. After all, it was the necessity of food that gave rise to the first spells, charms, blessings, and even the mythological origins of many deities. Food, in and of itself, was the impetus for the first magic. And though technology has evolved to the point where we don't need literal fire in order to cook our meals, whenever we stand over a piping hot stove we are still, ultimately, participating in the magic of the hearth.

THE KITCHEN WITCH

In many ways, the kitchen Witch of today is still attuned to the practices of the ancestors when it comes to food preparation.

These Witches may or may not grow their own food in gardens or on farms, or hunt or raise their own animals for consumption, but they do have an interest in and appreciation for the sources of their sustenance. Food is treated with reverence for the magical phenomenon that it is, and all aspects of its preparation are approached as ritual, rather than as household "chores."

In this way, even the implements and gadgets involved in cooking—such as spoons, pots and pans, cheese graters, and so on—are considered

magical tools. Practitioners of kitchen witchery will charge their ingredients with magical energy and focus their intention into every stage of the process when preparing food. They may create special dishes with specific magical intentions, or simply enhance everything they make with positive, divine energy.

Many kitchen Witches like to work "from scratch" as much as possible, avoiding processed and packaged foods in order to be closer to Mother Earth—the original source of all nourishment. But there are many different styles of kitchen witchery—as many as there are people who practice it—and no two paths are necessarily the same.

Generally speaking, kitchen witchery is a solitary path, and those who practice it may or may not also participate in a more "formal" path of magic such as those found in Wicca and other modern Pagan spiritual systems. In fact, many kitchen Witches do not practice other forms of magic, but keep their focus on the tangible world of the kitchen, where manifestation is always able to be experienced with the five senses and actually taken into the body.

They may incorporate specific rituals in their cooking—such as recipes and techniques handed down to them from generations past—or create herbal charms, medicines, and teas for achieving particular goals, but they don't necessarily work with any deities or make distinctions between ritual tools and everyday kitchen tools. In fact, plenty of these practitioners may not even consider themselves to be Witches or magic-makers, seeing themselves instead as simply being in tune with the natural energies of the Earth's abundant gifts.

For those who do practice Wicca or another Pagan path, the kitchen may be viewed as an extension of their magical practice, and even as a place where the more ceremonial or symbolic aspects of magic find tactile, three-dimensional applications. Here, the tools of ritual meet their practical counterparts: the chalice becomes a cup, the wand becomes a stirring spoon, the athame is now a chef's knife, and the cauldron is any pot with something simmering in it on a hot stove.

Recipes are spells, enacted not just in hope of magical manifestation but also for the purpose of enjoyable nourishment. Those who work with deities might devote some kitchen space to honoring relevant aspects of the Goddess and God—the supreme Wiccan deities—such as Cerridwen, a Celtic Mother goddess associated with grain, or Cernunnos, ancient god of the hunt.

Those whose practice emphasizes the Elements may focus on the roles that Earth, Air, Fire, and Water play in the process of growing, preparing, and eating food. And of course, Witches who celebrate the Wiccan holidays, or Sabbats, love to prepare feasts for these special occasions, using seasonally appropriate foods such as poached eggs for Ostara/Spring Equinox and root vegetable stew for Samhain.

There is no correct or incorrect way to practice kitchen witchery— it is a truly eclectic form of magic that can be shaped according to your own knowledge, intuition, and personal preferences. No special training or specific study is required. However, it can be very useful to have a working understanding of the inherent magical energy of food, especially for beginning kitchen Witches who are just embarking on their individual journeys.

Next, we'll explore a little bit of ancient mystical philosophy as it applies to the physical makeup of foods and how the act of creating and eating specially prepared meals helps bring about the positive changes we seek in our lives.

FOOD AND MAGICAL ENERGY

As we've discussed, the concept of food as a magical manifestation is not new. In fact, it has been with us since the days of our earliest ancestors. But aside from the fact that food comes to us through the abundance of Mother Earth, and beyond the rather miraculous process that allows us to start with mere seeds in a garden and ultimately end up with dinner, just what is it that makes food so magical? And how does what we eat become a means of magic all by itself?

There are as many frameworks for viewing the inherent magical properties of food as there are belief systems in the world, but the Hindu concept of *prana* is an especially useful one for today's culinary magicians.

Prana is viewed as universal energy, the vital life force running through all animate and inanimate matter. When we eat, we take into our bodies the prana of the individual ingredients, and this energy merges into our personal prana.

In Chinese traditional culture, the equivalent of prana is called *chi*, or *qi*, which literally translates to "air," or "breath," and has been described by modern practitioners of Traditional Chinese Medicine as the vital energy field that flows through and around living beings. Interestingly, the Chinese character for the word *chi* also has an implied meaning of "steam rising from rice as it cooks," which is a wonderfully appropriate image in the context of culinary magic!

Chi is actually known in various Asian cultures—as *ki* in Japan and as *khí* in Vietnam, for example—and many other cultures have a similar concept, such as the Hawaiian *mana*, and the Great Spirit found throughout the natural world in several Native American spiritual systems.

Food as Universal Consciousness

In Western mysticism, we find a few further concepts that can help broaden our understanding of this universal energy and the role it plays in the magical process, both in "regular" magic and in kitchen witchery.

For example, the Hermetic Principle of Mentalism, as found in the 1908 occult work *The Kybalion*, asserts that the Universe itself is one giant, interconnected mind. At its most basic level, all matter—both "living" and "nonliving"—is made up of information, or consciousness. All of creation is born out of consciousness, whether human-made creations like automobiles and skyscrapers, or natural creations like mountains, rivers, animals, and plants.

This consciousness is more evident in human beings and animals than in plants and inanimate objects, as the brains of living beings are directly interacting with everything around them (though plants also respond to their environments through sensory information).

But at the most fundamental level of the Universe, living beings are not separate or closed off from the inanimate world—all is consciousness, or, as *The Kybalion* states, "The All is Mind; the Universe is Mental." We can make a distinction between consciousness in thought form versus consciousness in material form, but the two interact with each other, as anyone who has worked a successful spell with any kind of magical tool can attest.

When it comes to prana or chi, these are viewed primarily as living energies, which fluctuate according to the exact physical makeup of a person, animal, or plant. Hindu Ayurvedic philosophy is partly concerned with the quality of the prana in the food we eat—just how much life force is in any given meal? Likewise, one of the aims of Chinese medicine is to raise or balance the level of a person's chi through adjustments to one's diet.

The implications for kitchen magic are that some foods have more potent universal energy—or consciousness—than others and are therefore more likely to bring powerful results. In view of this particular framework, you'll find general guidelines on pages 23–28 for choosing optimal ingredients for your magical culinary creations.

Eating as Transformation

Another Hermetic tenet that applies to kitchen witchery is the Principle of Correspondence. This is expressed in *The Kybalion* as "As above, so below; as below, so above," a phrase that has become part of many magical traditions.

In the classical model of this concept, "above" relates to the spiritual (or etheric) plane—the unseen level of reality that we don't perceive with our physical senses. "Below," then, is the material (or earthly) plane, where physical manifestations can be seen, touched, heard, smelled, and tasted. All creation begins as thought, or intention, which is sent out into the spiritual plane ("above"), made manifest, and then is brought into the material plane ("below").

These "planes" are essentially mirrors of each other, so that the change we seek happens at the very instant we visualize our magical request and send it out into the Universe. However, our human experience of linear time causes us to perceive the change as happening later, as it may take days, months, or even longer for the manifestation to become apparent in our lives.

We can see an example of this in the way the body interacts with the foods we eat. Whenever we make intentional choices about food—whether we're trying to lose weight, resolve a nutritional imbalance, or cure an illness—it takes at least a little bit of time to see results. The change we're intending for has already happened "above," but it has to work its way through the physical body "below" before we can perceive it for ourselves. This is true of magical work involving food as well.

However, when we deliberately channel our personal energy into the food we eat (and into the process of preparing it), we are likely to experience faster and more powerful results all around, as we have connected our conscious intent with the consciousness connecting the whole Universe.

Another way to explain the Principle of Correspondence is that what is true of the macrocosm (i.e., the entire Universe) is also true of the microcosm—or the Earth plane, where we experience our daily lives. This idea has been around in mystical circles since ancient times and has parallels to theories within modern quantum physics suggesting that at the most basic level, all matter in the Universe is fundamentally interconnected.

This can be a tough concept for the mind to integrate, as it truly runs counter to the way we perceive ordinary reality. After all, we see most things as being separate and distinct from one another, rather than being connected within an underlying energy field.

However, the phenomena of digestion and metabolism of food in the body can serve as an enlightening illustration. You've probably heard the saying "you are what you eat," but have you ever stopped to think about how literally true that is? Every nutrient the body takes in and metabolizes becomes physically part of the body's cellular structure. For example, vitamins from the baby spinach you added to your salad yesterday may now be fueling the cells in the bones of your fingers. The amino acids in the lentils you have for dinner tonight will help maintain your muscles tomorrow.

The body, as the "macrocosm," reflects the individual ingredients of every meal—or microcosm—that it absorbs and then transforms. When it comes to culinary magic, we take this transformational process to a whole new level—we are literally creating our bodies out of the conscious intentions we put into the food as we prepare it.

Food and Frequency

Because we *are* what we eat, whether or not we're actively working magic with our food, it's especially useful to keep in mind the Hermetic Principle of Vibration. Just as all matter is made up of information, or consciousness, all matter is also constantly in motion, in the form of vibration.

Of course, as humans we can only perceive a particular range of vibrational frequencies, so we don't recognize solid, stationary objects as vibrating. Nonetheless, at the subatomic level, every particle of matter in every solid object is actually in motion. It is through this motion that the consciousness of the Universe moves, connecting all things together at the most basic level of reality.

The Principle of Vibration is important to kitchen witchery in two primary ways. First and foremost, it's essential to understand that just as physical matter has a vibrational frequency, so does nonphysical matter, including our thoughts and emotions. Our very consciousness, in other words, is vibration.

If we are experiencing negative thoughts and feelings, our vibrational frequency is lower than if we are in a happy mood and thinking positive thoughts. Witches who succeed in magic do so because they make sure the energy of their consciousness is at a sufficient vibrational frequency to effect the change they're seeking.

If you're trying your hand at a love spell but feeling lonely and sad as you work, you're not going to manifest a fulfilling romance. Likewise, a money spell worked with a vibrational frequency of fear of not having enough is unlikely to bring anything other than a continued lack of money.

This same concept applies to the preparation of food—whether or not you're actively working magic. Indeed, both Witches and non-Witches alike

are susceptible to this basic universal principle of energy exchange. If you're angry or upset while you're making a soup, that energy will end up in the soup itself and is likely to cause some kind of discomfort for those who eat it, whether on a physical or emotional level.

The next time you find yourself feeling heavy or unpleasant in any way after a meal, reflect on how it was prepared. Were you eating at a restaurant where the employees are unhappy? If you ate at home, what was the vibrational quality of your energy while you cooked? Furthermore, did you take time to appreciate your meal and savor each bite? Or did you wolf it down while watching TV or texting on your phone? Just as the vibrational frequency of the preparation of food is important, so is your personal frequency during the experience of eating the meal.

If you think of it in terms of spellwork, eating can be compared to the sealing of a spell. You don't allow your focused energy to dissipate before lighting the candle, speaking the words, or whatever other sealing action the spell calls for. When it comes to food magic—and, arguably, eating in general—you get the best results by keeping a high, focused vibration from start to finish.

The second reason the Principle of Vibration is important is that each ingredient in your magical meal also has its own vibrational frequency. Therefore, some foods are higher in vibration than others, contributing to a higher personal frequency as a result; this is seen easily enough by comparing steamed vegetables and deep-fried vegetables. While the latter may be more appealing, depending on your personal preferences, the steamed version is definitely going to have a lighter impact on your digestion, resulting in a "cleaner," more high-frequency feeling after you eat.

This is because, as a cooking method, steaming allows the vegetables to preserve more of their prana (or chi), whereas deep-frying reduces this energy. This doesn't mean that you can't make a magical creation out of fried food, but it may mean that more of your own personal focused intention is required to bring the meal closer to the vibrational frequency of the healthier food.

So if you're just starting out with your kitchen witchery practice, you may want to begin with simple recipes that call for fresh, healthy foods. This will allow you to really notice the energy of each ingredient you're working with, as well as observing your own vibrational frequency before, during, and after your magical meal.

Keep in mind, however, that the quality of your focused intention is still the most important factor in any kind of magic. This makes it important to work with foods you truly enjoy. If you don't actually like the meal you're making, you're unlikely to summon the vibrational frequency needed to reach your magical goal while preparing and eating it.

OPTIMAL FOODS FOR A MAGICAL DIET

As any experienced Witch will tell you, your own personal energy and ability to focus that energy into your intention is the most important factor when it comes to any kind of magic. So again, when you're literally cooking up a spell, it makes sense to work with food you truly love. That being said, if you want to make the most out of the abundant gifts that Mother Nature has made available to you in your magical work, there are a few guidelines well worth keeping in mind.

Because different foods have differing amounts of prana or chi, choosing foods with the highest available quality of energy is ideal. We have seen that the vibrational frequency of any given meal affects us physically, mentally, and emotionally. This frequency is determined not just by the energy of the people involved in preparing the meal, but also by the ways in which the food is grown, harvested, and processed before you bring it into your kitchen.

The quality of the prana—the life force—in each ingredient has a direct correlation to the vibrational frequency of the meal as a whole. This life force is at its most vital in foods that have not undergone any processing before they are eaten. The more processing that takes place, the more prana is diminished. So fresh, whole foods that have been harvested very recently are the ideal ingredients—not just for magical cooking, but for your own personal vitality as well.

For example, a ripe tomato still attached to its vine is at its optimal state of living energy. As soon as it is picked, this energy begins to wane, as the tomato has been severed from its life-giving source. Of course, there is still plenty of prana within the tomato, allowing it to continue ripening on the shelf until it is eaten—either by you, by fruit flies, or by the microorganisms that will ultimately cause it to rot if it remains there too long.

People who love tomatoes will often simply cut these ripe, fresh beauties into slices and eat them raw, perhaps seasoned with a little salt and pepper. The deliciousness of this experience is due in large part to the high level of prana—and therefore the high vibrational frequency—of the tomato at this stage. Furthermore, the content of certain nutrients, such as vitamin C, is higher in the tomato's raw state than once you've cooked it, as heat further reduces the life force of any food.

Of course, this doesn't mean fruits and vegetables should only ever be eaten raw—in fact, there are other nutritional and digestive benefits of many foods that only become available through the cooking process. Indeed, the nutritional aspects of raw versus cooked foods are incredibly complex and are not necessarily important to consider from a magical framework. And given that kitchen witchery is all about the transformation of ingredients into a magical creation, the action of cooking is very often an integral step.

The point is that whether your food is raw or cooked, "fresh is best" in terms of vibrational frequency. The tomato you pluck from your garden or pick up at your local farmers' market is far more alive and potent than a tomato that spent a week on a truck, being driven hundreds or thousands of miles from its origin to your grocery store, losing more and more of its prana each day.

The fresh tomato is also higher in frequency than one that has been canned, no matter how fresh it was at the time of the canning process. The same is true for frozen vegetables and fruits—while they may still be of very high quality, they do lose vitality in the process of being frozen and then thawed.

Of course, it can be extremely difficult, if not impossible, to cook all of your meals without relying on any canned or frozen ingredients whatsoever—especially during the winter. So don't let a lack of availability of fresh foods stop you from creating the magical meal you're wanting to make. Just do your best to include as many fresh ingredients as possible, and look for high-quality canned and frozen produce when these items are necessary.

One way to maximize your use of fresh, locally available food is to eat with the seasons. If you follow a Wiccan or other Pagan path, you already do this to some extent at the Sabbats, as the feasts for these occasions always feature foods of the seasons in which they occur. But you needn't limit yourself to Sabbat celebrations when it comes to eating according to the Wheel of the Year. Instead, you can use the Wheel as a guide to magical menu planning throughout each season.

For example, the celebration of Lammas, or Lughnasadh, usually emphasizes summer squash and corn, among other foods. During the weeks of July through the end of August, or whenever squash and corn are locally available, you might try working food magic for enhancing your spiritual awareness, a magical goal associated with both. This is a great way of harmonizing your magic with the energies of the season, as well as working with the powers of the Earth in your own particular part of the globe.

In addition to freshness, another factor to consider is the methods by which the food you purchase has been grown. Over the past few decades, conventional, large-scale agriculture has come under increasing scrutiny when it comes to the use of pesticides and genetically modified organisms, as well as soil degradation due to monoculture farming, chemical runoff from fields into our water supply, and other practices that are impacting both humans and the Earth in alarming ways.

The widespread environmental damage associated with conventional agriculture is certainly at odds with the ethos of Wicca and other Pagan paths.

Even more to the point, however, the food produced by these methods is lower in prana, and therefore lower in vibrational frequency, than food produced in harmonious balance with the Earth. These days, more and more people are turning to organic produce, which as a result has become more widely available and more affordable than it was several years ago. Though still more expensive than conventionally grown produce, organic food is almost always of better quality and taste, and it is grown in a way that honors the natural processes of the life cycle on Earth.

This makes it a better choice not only for culinary magic, but for everyday eating in general. If budget concerns have kept you from buying organic foods, consider making a compromise by buying at least one or two organic items the next time you go shopping. You can do research online for the foods that have been found to contain the highest amounts of pesticides and other contaminants, and switch to organics for at least those items. The Earth will thank you, as will your body and your magic!

While your magical potential is ultimately only as limited as your imagination, there are some foods that are truly just not suited for kitchen witchery. Packaged and frozen meals, for example, don't really offer any opportunity for you to create anything—you simply pop them in the microwave or into a pot on the stove to heat them up. In addition, the life force in these foods is greatly reduced by the amount of processing they've been through (again, no matter how high quality the ingredients might be).

If you're in a pinch, you can add a little of your own magical energy to such meals by charging some fresh herbs to spruce up the pre-cooked food or putting together a quick salad to accompany it. (For instructions on how to charge ingredients, see pages 84–88.) By and large, however, any spellwork involving food should use fresh, whole ingredients as much as possible.

Choosing Magical Menus

When you think about all the possibilities that kitchen witchery presents, finding a place to start might seem a little overwhelming. Even if you have a specific magical goal, the options for incorporating it into a meal are pretty vast—especially if you're an experienced cook.

To help you narrow down your choices, try taking a simple approach: start with what you know and what you like to eat. Often, rather than having to seek out new recipes that fit with your magical goals, you can simply examine the correspondences of ingredients in dishes you already eat and tailor them to maximize their magical potency for manifesting your desire. You'll find examples of how to do this on pages 103–11.

One way to incorporate magic into your diet on a regular basis is to work with the season you're in. What's locally available right now? If you don't have access to locally grown food, think in terms of the next upcoming Sabbat before your next trip to the grocery store. Look to the traditional foods associated with that Sabbat and find (or invent) recipes featuring those foods. Then examine the correspondences or symbolic significance of the ingredients to see which of your current magical goals they align with, and take it from there—or you can start with the recipes in the Sabbat menus provided in Part Four of this book. (There are also a few resources for eating according to the seasons on the recommended reading list on pages 202.)

Whether or not you're a practicing Wiccan or incorporating spellwork into your meals, eating with the Wheel of the Year helps you attune on an energetic level with the turning of the seasons.

Along these lines, you can also work with the phases of the Moon, making food aligned with increase (e.g. prosperity, fertility) during the waxing phase and meals for banishing or decrease (e.g. healing from illness, resolving arguments) during the waning phase. Consider a monthly feast celebrating the current sign of the Zodiac with foods related to the strengths of that particular sign. If you're well versed in astrology, you can extend this approach to any significant planetary transits, trines, or other configurations, such as a meal focused on honoring Mercury in retrograde.

No matter how you go about planning a magical menu, always keep in mind that vibrational frequency is key to attracting the circumstances you desire. If you're forcing yourself to eat something you don't like, then you won't be at the right frequency for the spell to do its work.

On a related note, however, using magical correspondences and seasonal influences can be a great way to discover new foods that you've never tried before. Perhaps you want to make a magical meal to help you land a new job but can't find many correspondences among the foods you typically eat. This is an ideal circumstance for experimenting with something new.

When you find new foods that you like, there's an extra boost of joyful energy from your new discovery that can make for incredibly powerful magic!

The Vegetarian Question

The vibrational frequency of plant foods is, on the whole, much higher than that of meat, fish, poultry, dairy, and eggs. This may seem counterintuitive, since the level of universal consciousness within animals would seem to be higher than that within plants. However, the quality of the prana in animal-derived foods is greatly reduced by the manner in which animals are raised for consumption in the twenty-first century, particularly within the United States.

Most of the animals we eat have lived their entire lives in tightly enclosed, often dark, and very crowded spaces, which →

is counter to the way a living, breathing, conscious being is meant to spend its life. Many are fed or injected with hormones and antibiotics, resulting in food that is not really "natural" at all. This includes many fish farms. These practices diminish the life force within the meat that is produced, making it less efficient for magical purposes.

Furthermore, the environmental pollution that results from the heavily industrialized production (raising, slaughtering, and processing) of meat is not conducive to a harmonious relationship with the Earth. In addition, commercially wild-caught fish are quickly being depleted from our oceans around the world. These issues can be problematic for those Wiccans and other Witches who choose to work magic under the ethos of "harm none," since there is arguably a vibration of "harm" present in the energy of industrialized meat.

This information is not intended to be an argument for vegetarianism; what you eat is absolutely your own decision! As with any other form of magic, you should feel free to develop your own individual practice and to work with the foods you enjoy, no matter where they are sourced from.

On that note, it's worth mentioning that there are alternatives to "big agriculture" when it comes to meat consumption. There has been an increase in small, family-run farms where animals are treated with far more care and respect than those in the settings described above. Many of these farms are organic, and the meat they produce is on the whole healthier, higher in life force energy, and far less destructive to the environment. You may want to take a look around your area for local family farms, or ask at your local grocery store for more humane and environmentally sustainable options.

Finally, if you hunt your own game or go fishing in wild streams, rivers, or lakes, you will have a much stronger, more personal energetic connection to the animal(s) you bring home and the food you derive from them, just as our ancestors did. Working with food you caught yourself would arguably be the most potent choice available when it comes to meat and magic, as it gives you an opportunity to directly honor and give thanks to the spirit of the animal whose life you took.

This was an integral part of indigenous peoples' approach to eating meat, as the animals were generally respected as living beings in their own right. Just try to be cognizant of ecological sustainability—hunt during legal seasons and don't take more than you need.

Further Considerations

When it comes to maximizing your mastery of the magical energy of food, a few more tips are worth mentioning here.

First, understand that the methods you use in your cooking are as important as the ingredients themselves. The more hands-on, the better, as this is how you combine your personal energy with the energy of the ingredients you're working with. For example, if you're making a stir-fry, opt for chopping fresh vegetables yourself, rather than buying a pre-sliced frozen veggie mix. Or try making your own soup stocks rather than purchasing premade stocks.

Of course, most people don't have all day to make complex from-scratch meals, so make whatever concessions you need to in order to accommodate your personal circumstances. But as you begin to think of cooking as magical work, you may just find yourself making more time for doing things "the old-fashioned way."

One "rule" that is definitely recommended is to avoid using a microwave for any aspect of magical cooking. Although these devices have come a long way over the past few decades and are generally not considered to be unsafe

for our health as they once were, they still heat via radiation, which is not exactly compatible with the life force energy of the foods themselves.

If you're not convinced of this, try making a microwaved meal and a stove-cooked meal (of the same type of food) at the same time and see which one tastes more "alive." Even when it comes to boiling water, electric or gas heating is preferable to radiation. So if you've been in the habit of microwaving water for magical teas, consider getting an electric or stove-top tea kettle instead.

Finally, as a general practice, avoid wasting food as much as you can. Just as you wouldn't simply throw out leftover magical herbs, crystals, or other supplies, you want to honor the energy of your food by putting it to positive use. When it comes to perishable foods, buy only what you need (for help with this, avoid grocery shopping on an empty stomach!) or prep portions to freeze that you can easily defrost.

When planning menus, prioritize using up fresh food first, rather than leaving it to go bad in the refrigerator. Freeze leftovers or eat them the next day to take maximum advantage of their taste and nutritional value. And if you can, compost your food scraps, as this is a great way to thank the Earth for her abundance and to participate directly in the life cycle of the soil.

Being Practical

Hopefully, you now have a clearer sense of how food itself facilitates magical transformation, as well as how to approach choosing ideal ingredients for kitchen witchery. However, don't feel that you absolutely must grow your own food or buy only organic, local produce in order to work successful culinary magic.

While using fresh, healthy, prana-filled foods is always ideal, the single most important factor when it comes to kitchen magic is your personal energy—your vibrational frequency and ability to focus your intention.

So there's no need to completely overhaul your diet overnight. To do so would likely be more disorienting than useful when it comes to being centered in your personal power.

Instead, start with foods you know you enjoy and are comfortable preparing. If your go-to staples have always been of the canned or frozen variety, then by all means use them in your first forays into magical cooking. But make it a goal to gradually "upgrade" to fresher, more vibrant versions of these ingredients as you grow in your practice.

As you make this transformation, you will see the benefits—not only in terms of physical well-being, but on the magical level as well.

KITCHEN MAGIC FOR THE CULINARILY CHALLENGED

Generally speaking, most people would probably assume that those who practice magic—particularly any forms involving herbs and other natural ingredients—are at least decent hands in the kitchen, if not adept cooks.

This would certainly have been true for our ancestors, who would have at least had to know how to put a basic meal together, lest the family starve. Today, however, it is possible (and even common) to get by in life on microwaved food and takeout, so cooking has become much more optional.

If you're a Witch whose culinary skills don't go much beyond operating a can opener or slapping together a peanut butter and jelly sandwich, you might find the idea of kitchen witchery rather daunting. But don't be discouraged by any lack of experience. After all, even the most talented of chefs had to start from the beginning!

First of all, you can work kitchen magic with a can of beans or a simple sandwich. As with any other type of magic, the focus on your intention is far more significant than the specific objects you're working with. Often, the simplest spells have the biggest impact, as the lack of complicated ingredients and instructions makes it easier for the spellcaster to focus on their intention.

The same can be said for kitchen magic. In fact, one of the most commonly used forms of kitchen witchery—magical teas—is about as simple as it gets. As long as you can boil water, you can work a magical tea spell! So don't ever think you need to be a fancy cook in order to take advantage of the magic of food.

That being said, learning to cook from scratch is very much worth the effort, whether or not you're pursuing a kitchen witchery practice. As you learn to prepare your own food, you will feel more empowered to create change in your own life and experience improved energy on the physical, emotional, and spiritual levels. You'll also be deepening your relationship with the Earth, and therefore, your magic, no matter what form it takes!

The best way to approach learning to cook is to start simply. There are many cookbooks out there for beginners, featuring recipes with manageable steps and ingredients. And the internet is chock full of easy-to-find instructions for any question you might have. So start by finding some recipes that appeal to you—what sounds good to eat?

You don't even need to try cooking for specific magical purposes just yet. Instead, you might just focus on building a modest repertoire of meals you'll enjoy making repeatedly. In fact, if you pay attention to synchronicity, you may find that the food that appeals to you as you browse recipes is already associated with a magical goal or life improvement that would benefit you at this time.

Finally, allow yourself time to learn. Just as you can't become a magical adept in a matter of weeks, you're not going to be whipping out three-course meals right out of the gate. When you're learning a new recipe or cooking technique, try it out at least once before incorporating a specific magical intention into it. You need focus and confidence to successfully send out your intention to the Universe, so save the culinary spellwork for foods you can prepare without needing to pay attention to complex recipe instructions. Again, this doesn't mean that you should hold off on trying out kitchen magic until you've gotten the hang of actual cooking. While you're getting your culinary education, you can still practice kitchen witchery with meals you already know how to make.

ETHICS OF MAGICAL COOKING

Before we move on to the more practical sections of this guide, it's important to take a moment to examine the potential implications of working kitchen magic, especially when it comes to cooking for other people. After all, you can choose the most prana-filled, high-vibrational foods in the world and create the most intention-filled, magically focused meal you've ever made in your life, but if your motives aren't cleanly aligned with positive magic, you might be going to a whole lot of trouble just to end up with a whole lot of trouble!

When it comes to spellwork, the Wiccan philosophy states "harm none." On its face, this statement is self-explanatory, but it's important to note that "harm" also includes any form of manipulation attempted through magical means, no matter how innocent or benevolent the Witch's intentions may be.

This means that we don't attempt to lure a potential romantic partner with an aphrodisiac appetizer or get our boss to give us a raise by bringing them magically charged doughnuts. It also means we don't serve magical meals "on the sly" to friends and family members, even if the spell we used in the process is for excellent physical health or other positive intentions. Just as we don't work candle spells or make charmed herbal sachets for others without their permission, we don't do magical cooking without it, either.

Since we're dealing with food rather than other kinds of magical work, however, some ethical aspects of kitchen witchery can be a bit less cut and dried. For example, a mother of young children who have come down with the flu could certainly be in the right for adding extra healing magic to a brothy soup.

It's a different thing, however, for a parent to use magical food on a teenager in an effort to get him to clean his room, as this is interfering with free will. Of course, interfering with free will is often part of parenting, but when it comes to changing a child's behavior, the effort should come through communication, boundaries, and discipline rather than manipulative magic.

What if you're attending a potluck and want to charge up your contribution of pasta salad with vibrations of merriment for the occasion? (For instructions on how to charge ingredients, see pages 84–88.) In this situation, you just need to be clear and careful about your intention as you prepare the food. By all means, put your positive, joyful energies into each step of the process, but don't visualize the food itself causing the other people to be happy and have a good time.

Remember that it's enough to simply put your love into the food you offer to others, and that if you do so, they will always benefit from what you serve them. Anyone with a grandmother who baked the best pie on the planet or had the world's best chicken soup recipe will understand this basic truth: food created lovingly for others is its own magic—no spellwork required.

PUTTING IT ALL TOGETHER

So far, we've examined the roots of modern kitchen witchery, its ties with Wicca and other Pagan practices, and some of the esoteric theory behind the magical energy of food. Hopefully, those who are new to cooking in general have also gained some confidence about trying kitchen witchery and inspiration for choosing magically potent, prana-rich foods to incorporate into their practice.

In Part Two, we'll explore many practical suggestions for turning your kitchen into a sacred space and beginning to think like a magician in the culinary arena. And we'll take an in-depth look at one example of how you can apply what you've learned about the energy of food to the creation of a single, simple dish: magical marinara sauce. By the end of this next section, you'll be ready to start practicing kitchen magic on your own, even before you get to the kitchen grimoire in Part Three!

Part Two

THE WITCH'S KITCHEN

THE KITCHEN AS
YOUR ALTAR

S WE SAW IN PART ONE, OUR ANCESTORS MADE
the hearth the focal point of their homes, a place where
food was cooked and shared among family members and friends.

These days, an actual hearth is seen as something of a luxury, rather
than a standard feature of a home, and those lucky enough to have a
working fireplace don't tend to cook much over the flames. Instead,
modern technology has moved the preparation of food entirely to the
kitchen, and depending on the layout of the home, this may be where
meals are eaten, as well. In a sense, the oven and stovetop now serve as
the hearth, metaphorically standing in for the sacred fire that once
warmed everything—and everyone—in the home.

Viewed in this light, the kitchen as a whole can be thought of as a kind of altar, where sacred gifts from the abundant Earth are transformed into new creations that nourish and benefit the body. For the kitchen Witch, this metaphor becomes quite literal, as magical techniques are merged with culinary skills to manifest not just nourishing meals, but desired changes in one's reality. Of course, there's a significant difference between a kitchen and an altar you might keep for your ritual and/or magical practice: the kitchen serves many mundane purposes, while the altar is kept strictly for spiritual activities.

Depending on your living situation and your personal practice, you may or may not be able to treat your kitchen as an altar on an "all day, every day" basis. After all, it's not exactly easy to maintain a magical state of mind when you're rushing to make a quick breakfast before dashing out the door in the morning. Nonetheless, if you want to develop a successful kitchen witchery practice, it's beneficial to begin thinking of your kitchen as a sacred space—one in which magic can be worked at any time, for any purpose.

Throughout this chapter you'll find many suggestions for transforming your kitchen into a sacred space—a room-sized altar—no matter its size or current condition, and no matter whom you might be sharing it with. Creating your own Witch's kitchen will likely take a fair amount of work at the outset, but the effort will be well worth the magical experiences to come!

THE IMPORTANCE OF ENCHANTING YOUR KITCHEN

The Hermetic Principle of Vibration tells us that the subtle energetic aspects of preparing and eating food cannot be ignored if you want your kitchen witchery practice to be successful. The most crucial player when it comes to these energies is the person preparing the meal, as any negative emotions that are active within the cook are bound to end up in the food. Therefore, it's important to make sure you're in a positive mood when working your culinary magic, no matter what.

While this may seem like a tall order after a long, stressful day, it's usually not too difficult to transform your vibrational frequency if you're willing to let go of your less-than-pleasant state of mind. Treat yourself to a brief meditation session before you get started, smudge yourself with sage, or take a cleansing bath or shower if you have time. When it's time to cook, play music that puts you in a good mood and allow yourself to enjoy anticipating the delicious meal you're now preparing.

Setting your intention to have a positive experience in the kitchen is an excellent habit to get into, as your positive energy will contribute to more consistently enjoyable and successful cooking—whether you're preparing a magical meal, cooking for a Sabbat celebration, or simply making an ordinary breakfast.

There may be situations, however, where no matter how enthusiastic you are going in, your kitchen mojo just isn't where you'd like it to be. Perhaps you keep burning your pasta sauces or can't get the rice to turn out right no matter how carefully you measure the water. Maybe you keep dropping your stirring spoons on the floor, turning on the wrong burners on the stovetop, or setting off the smoke alarm just by making toast.

If you've ever had a run of bad luck in the cooking department, you're definitely not alone. Many Witches (and many more nonmagical types) have experienced what amounts to a "kitchen jinx" at one point or another. Whether it's that your meals just aren't tasting as good as you know they could or you're literally starting fires every time you try to cook, it's quite possible that the problem isn't your personal energy, but rather the energy of your kitchen.

Addressing Energetic Imbalances

Right now, if you can, go take a good look at your kitchen. (If you're not at home, close your eyes for a moment and visualize your kitchen as it looked when you last saw it.) As you stand in the center of this space, whether physically or in your mind's eye, how does your body feel?

Take a moment to check for any feelings of constriction or any other negative sensations. Now check in with your emotional state. Is there any anxiety, sadness, or frustration coming up for you?

If so, you're almost certainly picking up on an energetic imbalance within the physical space of your kitchen. And even if you're not noticing any particular sensations, it's still quite possible that your kitchen is in a less-than-ideal energetic state, especially if you've been plagued with any of the bad luck described on page 48. But there's no need to worry, as you can clear out any pesky "kitchen jinx" or other unpleasant energy with a good cleaning—on both the physical and ethereal levels.

As any sensitive Witch knows, physical spaces are repositories of nonphysical energy. This means that thoughts, moods, emotions, and energetic imprints of past events can linger within the walls of any space that isn't energetically cleared on a fairly regular basis. In other words, you don't have to live in a "haunted" house to have a kitchen in need of rebalancing.

In fact, any kitchen that hasn't been in use specifically as a "magical" kitchen before is almost certainly going to need an energetic overhaul before your practice can truly take off. This is especially true if you live in an apartment or house that has been rented by many different tenants over the years.

Does this mean you have to scrub your entire kitchen down from top to bottom? Well, if you want to maximize the magical potential of your kitchen witchery practice, then the answer is yes. But if you aren't able to dive right into a deep clean before you cook your next meal, there are smaller, less intensive methods for temporarily addressing energetic imbalances:

Declutter

Straightening up countertops, tables, and any other visible surfaces in your kitchen helps ease any underlying sense of chaos or disorder that you may not even realize is bothering you. This is basic feng shui 101 that is applicable to any room in your home, but it's a very effective practice in the kitchen and should ideally be done on a daily basis, especially just before you begin preparing a meal.

Sweep

Another practice to keep up daily if possible, sweeping the kitchen floor with a broom keeps energy from stagnating in corners and discourages Nature's little critters from venturing in to see what's for dinner. The broom is, of course, a signature symbol of the Witch, and its power to transform energy on a subtle level should never be underestimated.

If it's feasible, keep a broom specifically for your kitchen. This isn't strictly necessary, but it's nice to avoid mixing energies with any other rooms you sweep in your house. If you have a ritual broom or besom, you can also symbolically "sweep" your kitchen as an additional step, just as you would the sacred space where you hold magical rituals. (Of course, this doesn't mean actual sweeping—never let your ritual broom touch the kitchen floor!)

Smudge

Burning sage, lavender, rosemary, or a combination of these purifying herbs in a smudge stick will clear out leftover, unwanted energy from any space. If your kitchen feels particularly negative, however, you might want to try burning palo santo wood (*Bursera graveolens*), which works more specifically on darker energies. All smudging is more effective when the space has been cleaned, so do at least wipe down counters and sweep the floor before taking this step.

Leave a window or door open for the unwanted energy to escape through. If you're dealing with really tough negative energy, you may want to smudge daily for at least seven days to make a lasting impact. However, you'll still need to do a thorough deep clean of the kitchen in order to make a permanent improvement.

MAGICAL FOOD STARTS WITH A CLEAN KITCHEN

It's often said that truly good cooking requires making a mess. This may indeed be the case, depending on your style and approach to culinary creations, but beginning the process with a clean kitchen is always recommended. In other words, clean up the old mess before you make a new one.

Just as you wouldn't begin a new Sabbat or Esbat ritual without having cleared away any remnants of the prior ritual (on both the physical and ethereal levels), you don't want to start making a magical dinner while last night's dirty dishes are still sitting in the sink. So get in the habit, if you aren't already, of beginning your kitchen work with a "clean slate." You will find you get better results, especially when whatever you're creating is really important to you.

Taking this philosophy further, it really does benefit you to do a thorough, detail-oriented deep clean of your entire kitchen at least once a year. This means cleaning the inside and outside of your refrigerator, freezer, cupboards, microwave, any other frequently used appliances (such as blenders and coffeemakers) and yes, of course, your oven. You'll also need to clean under and behind everything that can be moved (including the oven and refrigerator) as well as all furniture, windows, and even walls—especially if they're painted and collect dust or grease over time.

If this sounds overwhelming, know that you don't have to do it all at once. Take it in stages, focusing on one area or appliance at a time. But do try to get it done within a few days, in order to really feel the benefits of the entire kitchen being sparkling clean all at once.

This is a perfect project to take on in preparation for the Sabbat of Imbolc (February 2 in the Northern Hemisphere, August 2 in the Southern Hemisphere), the traditional time when our ancestors would begin purifying their homes after being shut in over the long winter. But if Imbolc is a long way away, you certainly don't have to wait—feel free to start your kitchen deep clean today!

When it comes to cleaning supplies, be sure to show as much care and respect for the Earth as you can. Use all-natural cleaners whenever possible, and try to favor reusable cloths over paper towels. Avoid harsh chemical cleaners, as these are harmful both to people and the environment.

If you're dealing with an old, neglected oven with a ton of grime, you may need to make an exception, as all-natural products don't always get the toughest jobs done. As a general rule, however, remember that your kitchen is essentially an altar in and of itself, so unless they're absolutely necessary, chemicals and pollutants have no place there.

You can actually make your own cleaning products with essential oils, vinegars, baking soda, and other natural ingredients, which you can then magically charge with specific intentions, if you like. (For instructions on how to charge ingredients, see pages 84–88. Plenty of DIY-cleaning recipes are available with a bit of research, and you'll find a couple of examples on pages 55–56.

So when you're ready to completely overhaul the energy of your kitchen, put on some good music and make it as enjoyable as possible. As you sweep, wipe, and scrub away old dirt and grime, understand that you are also clearing out unwanted energy from your life. By giving this level of attention to your kitchen, you're making room for all kinds of goodness and joy—not just in terms of food, but also prosperity, love, health, and anything else you want to manifest in your life.

Mop the floor last, and then when all is dry and sparkling clean, give the whole kitchen a good smudge with one or more of the herbs mentioned on pages 50–51. You can then follow up by burning sweet grass or cedar to welcome fresh, harmonious, and loving vibrations into your newly enchanted kitchen.

Enchanted Kitchen Cleaners

Working with natural cleaning agents is a great way to enhance the vibrational frequency of your kitchen.

Start with base ingredients like vinegar, baking soda, and sodium borate (also known as "borax") and add the power of essential botanical oils to create fresh, pleasing scents and an extra boost of magical energy. If you like, you can tailor the recipes on pages 55–56 to create a specific type of energetic enhancement for your kitchen.

For extra magical "oomph," remember to charge the ingredients with your intention before mixing them together.

Essential Oils for Cleaning

Here are the physical and magical properties of eight essential oils you can use in natural cleaning mixtures depending on your needs:

BERGAMOT Antibacterial, positive energy, confidence, success, peace, harmony

EUCALYPTUS Antibacterial, protection, fresh energy

JUNIPER Purification, protection, healing

LAVENDER Antibacterial, purification, peace, harmony

LEMON Positive energy, purification

PEPPERMINT Antibacterial, purification, repels insects and mice

ROSEMARY Antibacterial, purification, protection

YLANG-YLANG Positive energy, peace, harmony

All-Purpose Kitchen Surface Cleaner

Spray down tables, countertops, stove tops, and other surfaces with this effective and delightfully scented concoction. Then just wipe with a cloth, allow the surface to dry, and you're done!

Ingredients

½ cup white vinegar	2 drops juniper oil	Clean spray bottle
1 tablespoon water	1 drops peppermint oil	Additional water as needed
4 drops lemon oil	2 tablespoons baking soda	
3 drops lavender oil		

- Add the vinegar, water, and essential oils to the spray bottle and swish the ingredients together to blend. Then add the baking soda, fill the bottle to the top with the additional water, and shake gently before use.

Natural Oven Cleaner

While this solution may not be quite strong enough to tackle a long-neglected oven, it should do the trick once you've given your oven a thorough deep clean with a conventional cleaner. For best results, wipe off any encrusted grease or food remnants with newspaper before applying the mixture.

Ingredients

2 cups hot water

1 tablespoon natural, chemical-free dish soap

1 teaspoon borax

3 drops lemon oil

2 drops eucalyptus oil

Clean spray bottle

- Mix all ingredients in the spray bottle. Spray liberally inside the oven and let sit for 20 minutes. Wipe off residue with a clean cloth.

KITCHEN ALTARS AND MAGICAL DECORATING

As discussed on page 46, the kitchen can be seen as an altar in and of itself. However, given that plenty of routine activities take place in this area of the home, it can be very effective to create a focal point for the specifically magical aspects of life in the kitchen.

A kitchen altar serves this purpose brilliantly. Here, you can keep any items that resonate with your kitchen witchery practice. This may include items representing the Goddess and God, such as candles, small statues, or paintings (see also pages 59–60). A small cauldron is an ideal symbol for a kitchen altar, as well as an athame (ceremonial dagger) and/or a chalice. You might also choose particular runes, hieroglyphs, or symbols from other esoteric systems that represent qualities you wish to attract to your kitchen practice, such as health, abundance, or success.

Depending on how much room you have, you may want to include a small potted plant or two. Edible herbs are a particularly appropriate choice (see also 58)—just make sure they get adequate sunlight. You can leave offerings of fresh-baked bread on your altar, place crystals associated with health and abundance around the perimeter, or whatever else feels appropriate. As with cooking itself, wthere are plenty of ways to be creative here!

You can dedicate one of your kitchen shelves to this purpose, or even use one of your cupboards if need be. However, if an altar isn't possible or just isn't a fit with your particular spiritual path, there are other ways of creating sacred space in the kitchen: hang charms for protection or good luck from the ceiling or on the walls, burn incense or magical essential oils, or simply keep a charged candle burning in a safe place while you cook. (A simple way to charge a candle is to lay it out under moonlight or on a moonlit windowsill; a Full Moon infuses objects with the strongest charge. Sunlight works as well, as long as it isn't so warm that it melts the candle.)

And whether you keep a permanent altar or not, always give consideration to the aesthetic quality of your kitchen overall. Keep things tidy as much as you can, so your focus isn't drawn to chaos and clutter when you walk into the room. Arrange dried herbs or pasta in attractive jars and keep unrefrigerated produce in hanging baskets or arrange them in some other pleasing way.

Plants

See your kitchen as a living, ever-changing symbol of the bountiful harvest and appreciate the evidence of abundance in your life on a daily basis. Doing so will help you maintain positive, harmonious vibrations throughout your kitchen. Plants, as inherently magical beings in their own right, are always appropriate for kitchen decor, and many can be used directly in your practice of culinary magic. Basil, for example, is a delightfully pungent herb that also lends your kitchen protection from negative energy. Rosemary is a hardy herb with a wide variety of magical and culinary uses. Really, any herbs that do well in pots, such as parsley, chives, mint, and thyme, are excellent additions to your kitchen "garden," as all culinary herbs have magical uses (see complete table of correspondence for culinary herbs on page 111).

Of course, not all of your kitchen plants need be culinary. For example, aloe vera—typically used for love, success, and lunar magic—can also offer protection against cooking mishaps as well as treat any minor kitchen burns or scrapes. Cacti, with their sunny, protective energies, are wonderful additions, provided they get plenty of sunlight. For kitchens with little sunlight, the protective and purifying properties of spider plants are a great alternative. And if you want to attract the magic of the faeries, be sure to hang a fern or two from the ceiling.

Crystals

Crystals are another great way to enhance the energy of your sacred hearth space. Place them on shelves, in cupboards, near the sink, or anywhere else where you'll see them regularly. Choose crystals that call to you, or look up stones with the magical properties of whatever you want to bring into your experience.

For example, amethyst's stress-relieving properties are helpful for transitioning from a long workday into a relaxed, magic-making frame of mind. Red jasper helps with the self-confidence and physical energy required to pull off a delicious magical meal. Citrine brings a sunny, abundant energy to your culinary work, while moonstone and blue topaz help to achieve and maintain a healthy diet. To enhance the well-being of your kitchen plants, bring in jade, moss agate, malachite, or any other green stones. And to enhance the taste of whatever you're preparing, keep a large quartz crystal near your oven.

Deities

For those who wish to work with ancient deities as part of their kitchen practice, whether as aspects of the God and Goddess or as separate deities in their own right, there are several possibilities to explore. As mentioned in Part One, the religious lives of our ancestors were inextricably bound with food and food production, so there are many, many deities associated with hearth and with agriculture.

Some of the most well-known hearth deities include the Greek goddess Hestia (and her Roman counterpart, Vesta) and the Celtic goddess of fire, Brighid, whose triple domains include smithcraft—forging tools in fire—and who is often associated with the cauldron. The Roman god Vulcan can also be considered a hearth deity, as he is associated with fire and creativity—both essentials for successful kitchen magic.

One of the oldest agricultural deities is the Greek Mother goddess Gaia, the personification of Earth who provides all sustenance. The Celtic god Bres, husband of Brighid, also governs fertility and agriculture. The Egyptian god of the Underworld Osiris provides food for his people through the growing cycles of the banks of the Nile. Ra, who is considered the father of Osiris in some Egyptian myths, is associated with growth as a god of the light and warmth of the Sun. The many grain deities of the ancient world include the Greek goddess Demeter and her Roman equivalent, Ceres, in addition to the aforementioned Celtic god Lugh.

Plenty of other pantheons, such as those of Asian, African, and Native American cultures, have such deities as well, and their primary associations can easily be found with a little research. If you're interested in working with any ancient deity, be sure to read as much as you can about them before attempting to form a sacred connection.

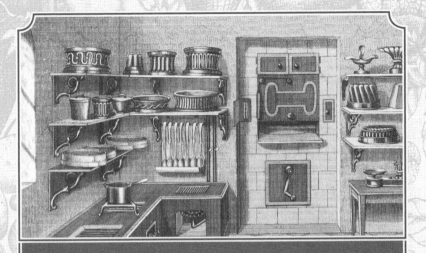

Enchanting the Tiny Kitchen

Studio Apartments and Other Tricky Kitchen Spaces

Arranging your kitchen for both optimal magic and ease of cooking can be a challenge even in the most spacious, depending on the location of appliances, cabinets, and other items. So what can you do if your "kitchen" is really just one corner of your studio apartment, or if it's a narrow space just big enough for a stove, sink, and refrigerator? It certainly can be difficult to feel truly free and in the flow of magical energy in such tight spaces. But you can still get creative with your tiny kitchen. →

If the kitchen is actually part of your living room, find a way to visually (and therefore energetically) designate the space. Perhaps you can paint the walls of this area a different color from the rest of the room, or place magical symbols and/or artwork on the cabinet doors. If you have to stand in tight spaces in order to cook, consider using small mirrors, à la feng shui, to energetically open up the space around you—you'll be surprised at the difference it makes!

Corner shelves are excellent space-savers in small kitchens and also potentially good places for an altar.

If you want an altar but have absolutely no space for a permanent one, find a small area of the kitchen that can serve as a temporary altar for when you're actively working kitchen magic—or create an "extension" of the kitchen by pulling a small table up to the entrance and placing your magical items there.

Many people with tiny kitchens find that cooking complex, from-scratch meals is highly challenging, if not downright impossible, due to limited space. If this is your situation, don't despair. As discussed in Part One, what matters most is your focused intention as you work, whether you're making a gourmet feast or a simple, humble meal. Like many aspects of the Craft, kitchen witchery is a very personalized and adaptable practice. Do what you can with what you have, and above all, enjoy yourself!

CONSECREATING YOUR KITCHEN

Depending on your personal approach to magic and your own spiritual path, you may wish to perform a consecration ritual on your kitchen, dedicating it to the purpose of co-creating with the Universe in the form of culinary magic.

If you're Wiccan, you likely already have a method for consecrating ritual tools, which you can modify for use on a whole room rather than on a single object. Your ritual will likely involve honoring the God and Goddess in your own way. The Elements may be invited to take an active role in the work, each bringing its characteristic energies to create a balanced magical atmosphere in your hearth space. Depending on your practice, you may even make the consecration itself part of a larger ritual within your tradition.

If you follow another spiritual tradition that incorporates the blessing of a home or a specific space, you could apply those practices to your kitchen. Or you can simply invent your own approach. You may write out an elaborate ritual, addressing each major aspect of your kitchen (such as the oven, the pantry, etc.) or you might keep it simple, with a few words of gratitude and intention.

As a very personal undertaking, your approach to consecrating your kitchen has to be something that resonates with you. To give you a possible starting-off point, an example consecration ritual can be found in Part Three on pages 98–101.

THE SHARED KITCHEN: "MUGGLES," CHILDREN, AND MESSY ROOMMATES

For single Witches who live alone, there is unlimited freedom to transform the kitchen into an ultra-magical space. For everyone else, however, it's often not that simple.

Those blessed enough to live with a magical partner or like-minded roommates may be able to engage their cohabitants to contribute to the effort, creating a truly magical shared creative space in the kitchen. But for the Witch who lives with non-magically inclined people, maintaining an enchanted kitchen takes a special kind of creativity.

Despite the progress the Wiccan and other Pagan communities have made in the last few decades in terms of being accepted (or at least tolerated) in mainstream society, many people on the path of the Old Religion still feel the need to keep their practices a secret, even (or especially) from other family members. This is often the case for those whose family, friends, or roommates belong to one of the Abrahamic religions (Judaism, Christianity, and Islam), and therefore may have misinformed views of the Craft.

If you are still "in the broom closet" when it comes to your spiritual practice, then how can you create and maintain sacred space in your shared kitchen?

First, know that you're in the company of generations who went before you, who lived and practiced in secret, and in extremely dangerous times at that. During the centuries when many Witches were executed for their way of life, anyone following the old ways had to keep their practice an absolute secret and likely would have hidden or disguised any tools of Witchcraft within their household.

This didn't prevent them from being able to work magic at the hearth, so there's no reason you can't do the same. The truth is, you don't absolutely need a physical altar or special symbols to imbue your shared kitchen with your own personal magical power. There are a number of ways to do so discreetly, without anyone in your household being any the wiser.

For example, you can certainly still clean your kitchen, holding the intention of clearing out unwanted energy while you work. If you have the house to yourself for a sufficient length of time, you can also bless the space with magical energy. Just be sure that your intention is not to manipulate the experience of others. Focus on enchanting the kitchen for yourself— the positive energy you create will likely have a beneficial effect on your housemates, provided you're not trying to make that happen.

You can also charge any object in the privacy of your room and place it in the kitchen as a talisman. (See page 57; the simple method described there for charging a candle can be used for other objects as well.) Depending on whom you live with, this could be a candle, a crystal, or a pretty stone you found while on a hike.

If even these items would raise eyebrows, try a houseplant, a knickknack, or a favorite mug—literally any ordinary object will do. It's great to be able to go all out and make your kitchen a total Witch's haven, but know that you can also achieve magical results with incredible subtlety. As with any other kind of magic, it's not about the material things themselves, but rather your own personal intention and will.

Those who live with young children will already be accustomed to keeping potentially dangerous things out of their reach, so this precaution can obviously be extended to any ritual items or other magical objects you don't want disturbed by curious little hands. You may want to devote a high shelf to serve as an altar, or install one if there isn't room on the shelves you have. And since you probably don't get a lot of time to yourself in the kitchen (as opposed to people without children), try involving the kids in your work.

Children have incredible imaginations and a ton of creative energy—why not harness that power by asking them to participate? Ask them to put their love and magical energy into the steps they help with, whether that's stirring, rolling dough, or even just "playing cook" with their own toys alongside you while you work.

What about that roommate who has a knack for creating a total mess in the kitchen right after you've just cleaned it? Depending on the social dynamic in your household, you may want to start by communicating your desire to keep a tighter ship in this regard. If you're "out" as a Witch, this will probably be easier than if you keep your practice a secret, since you can explain that the quality of energy in the kitchen will affect the quality of everyone's meals, and not just yours.

Of course, dysfunctional living situations, where roommates don't have good communication, are unlikely to change just because you want to improve the energy of the kitchen. Nonetheless, it's worth giving it a try. In terms of magical solutions, you can do spellwork for a cleaner, more energetically conducive-to-magic kitchen, provided you're not trying to manipulate the behavior of others in your household.

Spend time every day visualizing the kitchen as a clean, positive, and welcoming space without falling into resentment at the way it is now, and you'll be surprised at the changes that unfold.

Now that you've got your kitchen spick-and-span and blessed with magical energy, it's time to get out your culinary implements and start thinking and acting with a witchy perspective as you create transformative meals. On the following pages you'll find plenty of tips and suggestions for turning ordinary daily tasks into extraordinary magic.

MAGICAL THINKING: TOOLS AND TECHNIQUES OF KITCHEN WITCHERY

When it comes to thinking about magic, those who practice it as part of their spiritual path may automatically visualize an altar, ritual tools such as athames and pentacles, and/or the ingredients of spells such as oils, crystals, ribbons, and sachets. A successful practice of kitchen witchery, however, requires an ability to see the everyday objects found within the cupboards and drawers as also being magical.

Indeed, our ancestors made little distinction between the "magical" and the "mundane" when it came to acquiring and preparing food, and there's no need for a modern kitchen witch to make one either. Culinary magic is "practical magic" at its best, and once you learn to see every aspect of cooking with a magical eye, you'll be amazed at what a transformative process cooking can really be.

Reenvisioning Kitchen Tools

A great place to start is with the everyday objects and devices we use in order to prepare food. For those who work with ritual tools in Wicca or another Pagan practice, a few correlations will be fairly obvious, such as the chalice and the cup, the athame and the kitchen knife, the cauldron and the pot. However, anything you work with in the process of making meals can be viewed symbolically for an enriched, esoteric cooking experience.

For example, consider the simple skillet. Given both its shape and function, we can consider this tool to have feminine, receptive qualities, though there's also an emphasis on transformation through the masculine Element of Fire. The skillet evokes the process of necessary change—its contents are refined by the heat until they are suitable for eating. This way of conceptualizing the use of a skillet is good for culinary magic related to personal transformation and meeting challenges successfully.

Spoons can be thought of as a kind of wand, balancing the energies of a given dish through the act of stirring the ingredients together. Depending on your magical goal, you might choose to stir in a clockwise (or "sunwise" direction) for increasing or attracting something into your life, or stir counterclockwise for releasing or banishing.

A fork can be seen as piercing exterior illusions and getting to the inner aspects of a problem or matter. A colander filters out what isn't needed in a situation so that only the useful and desired aspects remain. Another fairly obvious equivalence is between the cookbook and the grimoire, or Book of Shadows. Both contain treasure troves of knowledge that can be referred to again and again for inspiration and technical assistance.

These are all examples of how you can stay in a magical state of mind as you work with your culinary tools to create edible magic. It's a metaphorical and essentially intuitive approach, and it works entirely on an individual level. Try reenvisioning your cooking methods through this magical lens, and once you find yourself making associative leaps, just run with it!

Tips, Tweaks, and Witchy Kitchen Hacks

Whether you're a beginning cook, a seasoned recipe-follower, or a maestro improvisational chef, there's always room to learn new methods and enhance your kitchen witchery practice. Here are a few suggestions for creative ways to take your culinary magic up a notch:

Substitutions and Additions

Depending on the type of food you're working with and your level of cooking experience, there are often opportunities to switch out or add ingredients to boost a standard recipe's magical power.

For example, you might use thyme instead of rosemary in a stew to boost psychic energy, or top a tray of roasted vegetables with chopped cashews to increase your income. Just be careful not to alter the taste of the food to the extent that you won't want to eat it, since you do need to enjoy the meal for it to have magical impact.

Water Work

Intentionally charged drinking water is a fairly well-known technique among Witches and other magical practitioners. Cooking involves the use of water so often that it seems a waste not to take advantage of this Elemental influence.

Get in the habit of blessing any water that will end up infusing the food somehow, whether it's for soaking beans, steaming vegetables, or cooking pasta, rice, or other grains. You can also charge herbs for your magical purpose and toss them into cooking water.

Using a few drops of a crystal elixir is another creative possibility. Just make sure you work with stones that are safe for the body. There are many crystals used in other forms of magic that are toxic when ingested, so do your research first!

Symbolism

Symbols are a central component in all kinds of magic—in fact, all magic could be said to work through the power of symbolism in one way or another. Try incorporating symbols into your edible creations where possible: carve dollar signs, hearts, runes, or other iconography into baked goods and "draw" symbols onto sandwiches and pancakes with ketchup, mustard, maple syrup, or other condiments and toppings.

You can also arrange appetizers and sides, such as crudités, chips, or fruit slices, into symbols on the serving plate. Taking this concept even further, you can use the symbolic power of numbers to enhance the experience of preparing and eating a meal. For example, sprinkle oregano into a sauce three times to honor the Triple Goddess, place nine cherry tomatoes on a salad for promoting growth, or ladle four generous spoonfuls of soup into each bowl to honor the Elements or celebrate creativity.

Keeping It Simple: Magical Flavor Boosts

Not every meal has to be an elaborate, premeditated magical production (although the results of such sessions tend to be well worth the effort!). You can integrate kitchen witchery into your normal cooking routine as well. Precharged creations like herbal tinctures, spice blend packets, pesto cubes, infused oils, and homemade salad dressings can be made ahead of time and kept on hand for spur-of-the-moment culinary magic. Add them to pastas, salads, soups, or whatever else you're cooking for an extra dash of magical energy on the fly.

Furthermore, if you're making a meal that includes more than one dish, know that not all of the dishes have to be dedicated to your magical goals. You can focus your intention into the salad or side dish that accompanies the main course, or even dessert. Kitchen magic shouldn't feel like an overwhelming endeavor—in fact, if it does become stressful, you're unlikely to get the results you seek. So take it easy, have fun, and do what you can as your schedule (and ability level) allows.

A MAGIC MODEL:
Manifest Your Goals with Magical Marinara

NOW THAT YOU'VE GOT SOME IDEAS FOR HOW TO transform your kitchen into a magical space, choose foods in accordance with your magical goals, and view the cooking process through a magical lens, it's time to look at a specific example of kitchen witchery.

Next, we'll take a fairly simple staple of Western cuisine—marinara sauce—and examine step-by-step how you can apply what you've learned so far about the magical energy of food and how to approach cooking from your new witchy perspective.

The first part of this section is not a specific recipe, but rather a set of broad guidelines for how you can select ingredients according to your magical goal, charge them with your personal energy, and put them to use in manifesting the change you're seeking, all while creating a delicious sauce for an enchanting meal. We do include an actual marinara recipe on pages 89–90 that you can use as a starting point if you wish.

MARINARA SAUCE BASIC INGREDIENTS

Marinara sauce is perhaps one of the most popular foods in modern Western civilization. It's also often referred to as "spaghetti sauce" because spaghetti is the pasta most frequently eaten with marinara, but you can actually use this sauce on any type of pasta, as well as on polenta and even on pizza. (In the case of pizza, however, the sauce is generally not cooked ahead of time.)

There is no shortage of recipes for marinara and there is plenty of variation among them, but in general, a sauce fitting the "marinara" category will be comprised chiefly of tomatoes with a handful of other ingredients for seasoning. (A "chunky" marinara may also contain additional vegetables for a more robust sauce.)

The relative simplicity of most marinara recipes, along with the opportunities to customize the sauce to your own liking—and your own magical goals—makes it a good dish to use as an illustration of magical cooking. So even if you're not a fan of anything remotely resembling Italian food, read on for a more in-depth sense of how you can use the principles outlined here in your own personalized kitchen witchery practice.

As you consider ingredients for your magical marinara, remember that "fresh is best" in terms of prana, or universal life force.

Depending on the season and your location, you may have access to incredibly fresh, locally grown, "high-vibrational" tomatoes as well as just-picked herbs and vegetables to create a delicious sauce from. (For example, there's a variety of hardy tomatoes known as "Mountain Magic" that has become increasingly popular at local farmers' markets!) On the other hand, you may need to rely on nonlocal produce or even canned tomatoes, which is perfectly fine.

In fact, if it's winter where you live, you might want to pass on any "fresh" tomatoes at your grocery store— especially if they're conventionally grown. These tomatoes have been picked too early in the ripening process, are often tasteless, and tend to feel very low-vibrational in terms of prana. So if these are the only tomatoes in your store, you're probably better off using quality organic canned tomatoes instead.

And if you're just not ready to try a from-scratch recipe for your marinara, there's no harm in using premade sauce from a jar! Just be sure to add your own magical touch to store-bought marinara by including fresh or dried herbs and/or other seasonings, focusing your personal energy into every particle of the sauce as you do so. Fresh herbs are wonderful when you can get them, but dried herbs are just as effective when it comes to magic, as any herbally inclined Witch will tell you. Whether your sauce is premade or homemade, you'll almost certainly want some combination of basil, oregano, parsley, thyme, and/or garlic.

If you're making your sauce from scratch, you may also want to include bay leaves, red pepper flakes, lemon juice, cornstarch for thickening, and sugar or honey to reduce the tartness of the tomatoes, as well as a chopped, sautéed onion. Additional vegetables you can add for a chunkier sauce include zucchini or summer squash, mushrooms, carrots, and bell peppers. (Note: you can also add veggies to a premade sauce by sautéing them first separately in olive oil until softened, and then stirring in the sauce.) We'll discuss the magical merits of each of these ingredients on pages 79–83.

If this is your first time making a from-scratch marinara, it's strongly recommended that you find a recipe to follow, such as the one on pages 89–90, so that your energy and attention can be focused on your magical techniques, with a fair amount of confidence that the sauce will turn out well!

CORRESPONDENCES AND MAGICAL GOALS

What is magical marinara sauce used for, in terms of kitchen witchery? There's no one single answer to this question, since there are many different magical properties associated with every ingredient you could possibly put in it.

For example, the tomatoes alone can be used in magic relating to love, protection, health, or money. If you choose thyme for a seasoning, you might draw on its associations with psychic awareness, purification, or attracting loyalty. Basil, on the other hand, can be used for prosperity or protection.

This diversity within the magical energies of food is at the heart of the creative potential of culinary magic. It's also part of what makes it so practical! With this variety of possibilities in mind, let's take a look at some of the known magical correspondences for each of the ingredients you might include in a marinara sauce:

Vegetables

BELL PEPPERS Green (prosperity); red (vitality, strength); yellow (creativity)

CARROTS Vision, sex, masculine energies

GARLIC Health, protection, banishing, breaking hexes

MUSHROOMS Psychic awareness

ONIONS Protection, prosperity, clearing away obstacles

TOMATOES Money, health, attracting love, protection

ZUCCHINI/SQUASH Spirituality, fertility

Herbs and Spices

BASIL Money, loving vibrations, protection, warding off negativities in a home

BAY LEAF Good fortune, money, success, protection, purification, strength, psychic awareness

OREGANO Peace, deepening love relationships, releasing old relationships

PARSLEY Protection (specifically from accidents), money, luck, lust, strength, vitality

RED PEPPER FLAKES Deflecting negative energy, avoiding unpleasant people

ROSEMARY Purification, health, love, energy, mental clarity

THYME Love, affection, attracting loyalty, courage, psychic awareness, purification

Other Ingredients

CORNSTARCH Protection, harmony with Earth, luck, abundance

HONEY Health, happiness, love, lust, sex, purification, wisdom, stability

LEMON JUICE Love, longevity, purification, marriage, happiness, faithfulness

OLIVE OIL Peace, health, protection, spirituality, sex, fertility, fidelity

RED WINE Celebration, relaxation, gratitude, appreciation

SUGAR Love, affection, banishing gossip

As you can see, there are many different goals you could focus on as you create your magical marinara. However, some goals have a greater likelihood of success than others, depending on the magical properties of all the ingredients you choose to include.

For example, yellow bell peppers are associated with creativity, and adding some chopped yellow pepper charged with this intention could certainly have an impact. But if your desire is truly to increase your creativity, then it might make more sense to create a dish that features yellow peppers and/or other foods associated with creativity more prominently than a marinara sauce typically would.

Indeed, focusing on a goal that's represented in as many ingredients as possible is ideal for maximizing the meal's magical energy. And since the main ingredient in marinara sauce is tomatoes, it makes the most sense to work for a goal associated with one of the magical attributes of tomatoes. With this in mind, let's look at how you might concoct a magical marinara for the purposes of manifesting money, health, love, or protection.

If your intent is to attract money, you'll definitely want to include basil and parsley in your sauce, as well as a bay leaf or two. Onions and green bell peppers are also good additions here, as is zucchini squash, with its green color and association with fertility, which can be applied to one's business or investments.

For health-related goals, be sure to use plenty of garlic and olive oil, and consider sweetening the sauce with a bit of honey. In addition, a quick squeeze of lemon juice, for longevity, helps bring out the flavor of the tomatoes.

Of course, it's worth noting here that any food that is high in prana and prepared with positive intention is suitable for health-related goals, since what we eat is a primary factor in our overall health. However, it can still be fun to zero in on foods traditionally associated with good health when it comes to magical dishes.

When it comes to love-related goals, you can choose ingredients according to the particular situation you're wanting to attract. Thyme and basil are excellent for bringing the energies of love and affection into your life, while parsley, carrots, and olive oil are more associated with lust and sex. Olive oil is also known for encouraging fidelity, and oregano is used for releasing old relationships and strengthening existing ones.

The sweetness of sugar makes it probably the most obvious of love-associated ingredients, and it can be used here to temper the acidity of the tomatoes. (Raw or brown sugar is recommended over refined white sugar.) Honey is an excellent alternative to sugar, as it also has associations with love, as does lemon juice, which is often found in recipes for marinara and even in many brands of canned tomatoes.

While bay leaves are not primarily associated with love, they are associated with success and good fortune. This makes them great all-purpose magical ingredients—simply charge them with your specific intention, and let their magical energy infuse the sauce!

Many of the ingredients discussed here so far are also associated with protection. In addition to the tomatoes, we find protective qualities in basil, parsley, bay leaf, garlic, olive oil, onion, and even cornstarch. As with love-related goals, you can do some further research to tailor your choices to your specific circumstances.

If you're seeking protection from accidents, use parsley. If you're warding off illness, use garlic. Garlic is also good for protection from unwanted energies in the home, as is basil. There are other protective herbs and seasonings not mentioned above that can also go well in a marinara sauce, such as salt, black pepper, and marjoram. Each of these has their own particular "flavor" of protective energy, guarding against a range of unwanted experiences, from general negativity to jealousy to theft.

Another option in a customizable dish like marinara sauce is to work with the magical associations of a key secondary ingredient, with the intention that the energy of the ingredient (as well as other complementary ingredients) becomes the magical focus of the meal.

For example, if you want to make a sauce that emphasizes mushrooms, you could decide to focus on the psychic energies of these delectable edible fungi. Include a bay leaf and some thyme, and you've got three ingredients associated with boosting psychic awareness.

As you can see, there are many options for choosing a magical goal for a dish with multiple ingredients. All it takes is a little research into magical correspondences along with your own creativity and intuition.

As for what you'll be serving your marinara with—whether it's pasta, polenta, or something else—this is, of course, entirely up to you. Depending on your purposes, you may see this component as an integral part of the overall magical dish, or you may focus your intent into the sauce alone, which will then cover whatever is served underneath it. This is a perfectly fine approach—not every single part of a given meal needs to be magically prepared.

However, you might enjoy incorporating, for example, the traditional Chinese association between long noodles and long life, luck, and success into your dish. Others have associated spaghetti and linguini with protection, while spiral pasta is said to enhance creativity. If your goal is a new job or business opportunity, try using bowtie pasta. If you're more of a polenta person, you could draw on any of the magical properties associated with corn, such as protection, luck, abundance, or divination, just to name a few.

Finally, when it comes to choosing ingredients, this bit of advice is worth repeating: make sure you enjoy what you're preparing! This is crucial to the success of your magic. If you're working for prosperity but hate green peppers, then by all means leave them out of your marinara sauce, regardless of the correspondence. You can focus your intention on the money energies of the basil, parsley, bay leaf, and so on, instead.

CHARGE, COOK, ENJOY

Once you've decided on a goal for your culinary magic and the specific ingredients for your dish, you're ready to put your kitchen witchery into practice.

First, always be sure to "set the stage" for magic, just as if you were preparing for a ritual or other types of spellwork. Light a candle or two and put on some inspiring music. You might want to light some incense or place a few drops of essential oils on an oil burner. Spending a few moments quieting your mind and letting go of your day is essential, especially if you've been busy or under any stress. Do whatever you need to do to create for yourself a sense of ease and wonder as you transform an otherwise basic household chore into a magical experience—remember, your kitchen is now an enchanted space! And just as you would gather your ingredients prior to spellwork, be sure to get out everything you need for preparing the meal—including all kitchen implements and cookware—so you won't be interrupted in your magical focus by having to dash for something at the last minute.

Now it's time to charge your ingredients. There are many ways to do this, and you may already have your own preferred method(s) based on your personal experience with spellwork.

When it comes to kitchen magic, one very practical way is to simply hold the ingredients between your palms. This works particularly well with fresh vegetables and fruit, as their relatively high water content, in addition to their high degree of prana, makes them very receptive to absorbing your energy.

Take a deep breath, and as you exhale, visualize your personal energy infusing the food with your magical intention. You might also visualize a specific color in association with your goal flowing into the item, such as green for prosperity or orange for courage, or you might simply call upon the prana of the food to connect with you and your desire. You can do this silently, or you can speak some brief words aloud. For example:

"I call on the life force energy of (name ingredient) to assist me with manifesting (name magical goal)."

If you're using canned tomatoes, simply hold the can between your palms and send your energy into the food within. (Whenever possible, remove the lids of cans, jars, and bottles for closer energetic proximity to the ingredients within.) If you're using a premade sauce, then hold the jar and visualize each of the ingredients being activated with your personal power.

You may wish to acknowledge each ingredient according to its role in your spellwork—for example, tomatoes for promoting good health and garlic for protection from illness. As with any other aspect of magic, this is all entirely up to you and what feels appropriate in your experience. In fact, the specific approach you use for charging ingredients is not important at all—all that matters is your ability to focus your personal magical energy into the food for its intended purpose.

If the prospect of charging each and every ingredient before the cooking begins to sound daunting, know that in most cases you can actually do this step in advance. Just as you might need to charge crystals or candles a day or two ahead of a Full Moon spell, time constraints might require you to charge ingredients for magical meals when you bring them home from the grocery store.

This is fine, though some people like to hold off on charging fresh produce until after they've rinsed it to keep as much of their energetic imprint on the food as possible. Furthermore, you don't have to individually charge every single item—holding a handful of tomatoes or a few cloves of garlic and charging them all at once is perfectly effective.

Remember, ultimately this process should be enjoyable, rather than tedious. Keep your focus on maintaining a high vibrational frequency and approach each magical action in a way that delights you.

Once your ingredients are charged, proceed with making your marinara as you normally would, but with a continued focus on your magical goal. If you're slicing vegetables, for example, you might envision the energy of each slice infusing the overall sauce with its inherent magical vitality. If you're adding multiple herbs to the sauce all at once, place them in a bowl or mortar first and mix them together with your fingertips—this is a particularly powerful step in many herbal spells. If you're sautéing onions for the base of the sauce, visualize the magical energies of olives and onions fusing together and strengthening the potency of the dish.

If you like, speak spell words, incantations, invocations to the Elements, or anything else that fits your magical style. Do the same with any other vegetables you add, as well as with herbs, sugar, or other additions to the marinara—each item you bring into the mix is adding its own energies to create a nourishing, delicious manifestation of your desires.

You can make this process as simple or as elaborate as you like—the important thing is to stay focused on your goal from start to finish. Don't be running through the details of your day or worrying about the future—stay in the present moment. And be sure to taste the food as you go, noting the changes made by each addition to the sauce and appreciating the ongoing transformation of these raw ingredients into a magical meal.

If you're using a premade jar of marinara, then obviously you don't have as many opportunities to visualize your intended manifestation during the cooking process. But this doesn't mean you can't infuse your meal with magic all the same.

First, as mentioned on page 78, add your magical energy to the jar of sauce before beginning your work, visualizing each of the ingredients being infused with magic. Then pour the sauce into a saucepan and heat it up gently. (If you're adding vegetables, sauté them in olive oil first, visualizing intently as you do so.)

Even if the sauce already tastes great, be sure to add something to it that you've charged with your magical intention—whether it's fresh or dried herbs, sugar, honey, or lemon juice—to punch up the flavor. Make it as much of an original creation as possible—you can even drizzle some magically charged olive oil over some fresh crusty bread to accompany your meal.

Magical Marinara Base Sauce

This master recipe can be followed as is or used as a starting point for creating your own unique magical marinara.

Makes about 8 cups (2 l)

2 tablespoons extra-virgin olive oil

1 large yellow onion, diced

6 cloves garlic, coarsely chopped

Pinch red chili flakes

2 large sprigs basil, left whole

3 bay leaves

2 tablespoons tomato paste

1 cup (237 ml) red wine

3 pounds (1.35 kg) ripe heirloom or mixed organic tomatoes, cored and coarsely chopped

1 28-ounce (794 g) can organic chopped tomatoes

1 cup coarsely chopped fresh parsley (including some stems)

1 tablespoon dried or 2 tablespoons chopped fresh oregano

1 teaspoon dried or 2 teaspoons chopped fresh rosemary

kosher salt and freshly ground black pepper, to taste

- Heat the oil in a stockpot or Dutch oven over medium-high heat. Add the onions, garlic, chili flakes, basil, and bay leaves, and cook, stirring frequently, until onions are very soft and beginning to brown, 6 to 8 minutes.

- Stir in the tomato paste until the vegetables are coated; cook, stirring, until the paste begins to brown, about 1 minute. Stir in the red wine and bring to a simmer; scrape the bottom of the pot to release any browned bits. Simmer until the liquid has reduced by half; add the chopped fresh and canned tomatoes, parsley, oregano, and rosemary. Bring the mixture to a boil; reduce the heat to a simmer, cover, and cook, stirring occasionally, until the tomatoes have completely broken down, about 40 minutes.

- Remove the bay leaves and, working carefully in small batches in a jar blender or immersion blender, puree the sauce. Alternatively, you could use a potato masher to mash the mixture by hand until as smooth as possible. (If using a potato masher instead of a blender, remove the basil stems first.) Taste and season with salt and pepper.

- If the sauce is too thin, continue simmering to desired consistency or whisk 2 teaspoons cornstarch into some red wine or water and add it to the sauce; bring to a simmer and cook until thickened. If the sauce is on the sweet side, add a squeeze of lemon juice. If too acidic, stir in a teaspoon or two of honey.

When your marinara is ready (along with the pasta or whatever it is you're serving it with), it's important to take a moment to truly appreciate your magical creation before digging in.

If you already have a tradition of praying over your food before you eat, then this step is already built in, but if not, be sure to incorporate a statement or two of gratitude into your kitchen witchery practice. You might wish to acknowledge the Goddess and God or the Elements, and say a few words about the magical goal you're seeking to manifest. Or you could keep it simple with something like the following:

"I give thanks to the bounty of Mother Earth for this life-giving and transformative meal. Blessed Be."

As you eat, be sure to appreciate the taste of the food and the magical work it's accomplishing, and appreciate yourself as well for putting in the time and effort to create the meal. Stay focused on this enjoyment, remembering the importance of vibrational frequency to magical work. Don't eat in front of the TV or scroll through messages on your phone while you eat—be present with your food. Keep mealtime conversations pleasant; avoid complaining about your day or gossiping, which will lower your vibration and weaken the spell.

When you're finished, it's a good idea to "seal" your culinary spellwork with an acknowledgment of the physical processes of digestion, here on the Earth plane, that contribute to the manifestation of your goal. For example, since digestion involves each of the Elements, you might say something like this:

"By the powers of Earth, Water, Air and Fire,
I now manifest the goal that I desire."

You could also tailor these words more specifically to the goal you're working for, if you like. The main thing is to mentally connect, one final time, the magical energy of the food you've prepared and eaten with the energy of your physical body. From an esoteric perspective, this simple act of creating a nourishing dish with focused intention—whether it's marinara, beans and rice, or broccoli casserole—is a very practical way to employ the Hermetic principles discussed in Part One. By choosing as many fresh, high-in-prana ingredients as possible (and choosing high-quality canned/packaged foods when necessary) and keeping a cheerful, relaxed mood throughout the process, you are utilizing the Principle of Vibration to your best advantage.

Likewise, by focusing on your intention as you charge the ingredients, and visualizing your desired outcome with each step of the cooking process, you are connecting yourself and your goal with the Universal mind via the Principle of Mentalism. Finally, by eating and enjoying the meal you are taking in the inherent magical properties of specific foods (the microcosm) and incorporating them into your body (the macrocosm) to obtain specific results—an excellent way to employ the Principle of Correspondence.

But whether these specific concepts ever cross your mind while you're in the kitchen doesn't actually matter. As long as you're focused, energized, and having fun, you're bound to experience success in your practice of culinary magic!

MOVING FORWARD WITH YOUR PRACTICE

Hopefully, the discussions above regarding enchanting your kitchen and reenvisioning the cooking process, as well as the master example of magical cooking, have given you a sense of the endless possibilities and potential for creativity when it comes to kitchen witchery.

In Part Three, you'll find even more inspiration for transforming the mundane into the magical, including a few sample recipes; spells for enhancing your practice; tables of correspondence for basic pantry staples, common food colors, and Elemental influences; and further miscellaneous ideas for making the most out of the magical energies of your food.

Part Three

A KITCHEN
GRIMOIRE

BLESSINGS AND RITUALS
FOR THE MAGICAL COOK

C ENTURIES BEFORE WICCA AND OTHER MODERN forms of the Craft came into being, magical texts were often known as *grimoires*. These books, often handed down from one generation to the next in secret, contained spells, rituals, and other magical information sometimes dating back to ancient times.

Cookbooks also have an ancient lineage. Many early cookbooks included both culinary recipes and magical information—from herbal potions to medicinal charms—since food and magic were not seen as separate domains until just a couple of centuries ago.

The collection of information on these pages is a mini version of what an ancient culinary grimoire might have contained, though very much updated for the modern world. Use it as a starting point for creating your own personal magical cookbook, adding and changing details as you experiment to find what works best for you.

Elemental Kitchen Consecration Ritual

Here is an example consecration ritual that can be used by Wiccans and non-Wiccans alike.

The universal energies of the Elements are called upon to enhance the magical atmosphere you'll be creating in your kitchen. If you wish, you can also include language that incorporates the Goddess and the God or any other deities you have a spiritual connection with.

It's best to perform this ritual after a thorough deep clean of your kitchen, but if that's just not possible, don't let it stop you—just clean as much as you can beforehand. Smudge with sage, rosemary, or lavender before beginning the blessing.

The herbs suggested for this ritual all double as kitchen spices and are associated with purification, protection, good luck, and/or success. The list of options is not remotely exhaustive, however, so if there are other herbs you'd prefer to work with, by all means do so!

Depending on the layout of your kitchen, you may not be able to place each Element candle directly on the floor in the center of each wall. If this is the case, just place the candle as close to this spot as possible, even if it has to be on a countertop, a shelf, or even on top of the fridge.

Materials

White spell candle

Fire candle (red or orange)

Earth candle (green or brown)

Water candle (blue or silver)

Air candle (yellow or white)

Consecration incense in an incense burner or a few drops of essential oil in an oil burner or heated diffuser, with one or more of the following ingredients:

- Frankincense
- Jasmine
- Cinnamon
- Myrrh
- Rose
- Lavender
- Sandalwood
- Ylang ylang
- Lemon

4 bay leaves (good fortune, success)

1 whole cinnamon stick (consecration, success)

1 whole star anise (consecration, purification, luck)

1 teaspoon each of four of the following herbs:

- Clove (protection, good luck)

- Basil (purification, protection)

- Cumin (protection)

- Dill (protection)

- Fennel seed (purification, protection)

- Rosemary (purification, protection)

- Thyme (purification)

4 small token representations of foods you really like: e.g., a pinto bean, a dried cranberry, a piece of dry pasta, a small piece of bread

Mortar or bowl

Ritual

Gather all your ingredients and place the incense or essential oil and the white spell candle on a surface that serves as a focal point—your kitchen altar, if you have one, or a table or countertop.

Take a deep breath, exhale, and light the incense or oil.

Place each Element candle on the floor at the center of the wall that most closely aligns with its directional association, in the following order: Earth in the north, Air in the east, Fire in the south, and Water in the west.

Now, light the Earth candle and place a bay leaf in front of it. Do the same with the Air, Fire, and Water candles.

As you do so, verbally acknowledge the power of the Element as it relates to food and food preparation in the home using the following (or similar) words:

Earth: *"I welcome the energies of abundant sustenance into my kitchen."*

Air: *"I welcome the energies of the invisible life force into my kitchen."*

Fire: *"I welcome the energies of nourishing transformation into my kitchen."*

Water: *"I welcome the energies of life-sustaining flow into my kitchen."*

Next, place the four teaspoons of your chosen herbs in the mortar or bowl.

Mix the herbs together with your fingers and then stir them with the cinnamon stick three times in a clockwise (sunwise) direction.

Briefly dip each food token into the herb mixture and place it on one of the bay leaves.

Briefly dip the star anise into the herb mixture, and then place it in front of the white spell candle.

As you prepare to light the candle, take a deep breath, exhale, and say the following (or similar) words:

> *"Working in union with the powers of Earth, Air, Fire, and Water,*
> *and with the sacred Fifth Element of Spirit,*
> *I bless this kitchen."*
>
> *This room is now my sacred hearth space*
> *where magic is made with joyful intention,*
> *nourishing the body, mind, and soul.*
>
> *Blessed Be."*

Now light the white candle and spend a few moments in quiet reflection.

When you feel that the consecration work is done, take the food tokens, bay leaves, and herb mixture outdoors and sprinkle them over the Earth.

The star anise and cinnamon stick can be used later in magical recipes or kept as lucky kitchen charms. The Element candles can be gently extinguished and used again in other ritual work or just for ambience. Leave the white spell candle to burn out safely on its own. (Remember to never leave candles unattended.)

WORKING WITH MAGICAL
CORRESPONDENCES

A S HAS ALREADY BEEN NOTED SEVERAL TIMES IN this book, your focused intention is the most important factor in the success of your magic. You will be infusing the individual ingredients of the meal with your own magical energy, no matter what the ingredients are or how you're using them in the work.

However, just as with spellwork, you can enhance the results of your culinary magic by choosing foods according to their magical associations, or correspondences. Just as you might work with patchouli oil—with its magical energies of prosperity—in a money spell, you can use barley, basil, and/or pine nuts in a casserole dish to bring about the same results.

So how do you discover the magical correspondences of any given food? Research is always a good idea, but your own intuition should always be the final judge.

Magical correspondences come to us from ancient mythology and legends, as well as family traditions, medicinal knowledge, and personal experience. To take a random example, avocados are magically associated with love, lust, and beauty and are used in spellwork to bring about or enhance these qualities in a person or a relationship.

This correspondence is likely connected to the belief systems of ancient Aztec and Mayan cultures associating avocados with the powers of attraction. One Aztec legend tells of how young, beautiful unmarried girls were kept indoors during the height of avocado season to keep them sequestered from men who were under the aphrodisiac spell of these rich, delicious fruits.

In early Western medicine, a concept known as the Doctrine of Signatures held that every plant that was useful to the body had a physical resemblance—or correspondence—to the part of the body it could heal. For example, the walnut has an uncanny resemblance to the human brain, and is widely known today to be highly beneficial to brain function.

The original Greek name for the walnut is *caryon*, meaning "head," and magical associations for this nut include wisdom and the conscious mind.

When it comes to discovering correspondences, there are plenty of online resources to consult, as well as a few trusted print sources that will be listed on the recommended reading list on page 202. Having this ancient wisdom at your fingertips is of great help as you build your kitchen witchery practice. However, the correspondences listed for any given food can vary from source to source, and ultimately the foods you choose to work with should make sense to you personally.

Don't feel that you need to use a specific ingredient just because a source you've consulted connects it with your goal. If you trust the source, great—that may be enough in many cases. But if you don't have a connection to the correspondence within yourself, the visualization/focused intention level isn't as strong.

In other words, if you're seeking new sources of prosperity, and your gut is telling you to make a carrot and sage soup, then by all means do so, regardless of whether you can find confirmation of this correspondence elsewhere. As you deepen your practice of kitchen witchery, you will likely start to intuit the best foods to work with at any given time, rather than having to do research for every magical meal.

One way to start building your own personal understanding about correspondences is to hold a food item in your hands and listen to what your intuition tells you regarding its ideal magical uses. You can also peruse your pantry with your magical goal in mind and see which items immediately catch your eye. Just as experienced Witches find that specific herbs and crystals "speak" to them when they're looking for ingredients to create a particular spell, you'll likely find that certain foods in your pantry call to you when they are most likely to be useful in your magic.

If you want to take a simple but effective approach to correspondences, consider working according to the colors of different foods. You might use red and orange items (such as bell peppers and carrots) for work related to courage, strength, and vitality; green foods (like spinach or snap peas) for prosperity; and purple foods (like cabbage or eggplant) for peace or wisdom. For more on this, see the table on pages 108–9.

Finally, if you already have personal established correspondences between certain foods and aspects of life, then by all means work with them. You might, for example, associate cherries with wisdom or familial love if you had a wise grandmother who made cherry pie for you when you came to visit her. Or a favorite food discovered on a vacation might be permanently connected to feelings of joy, freedom, or enlightenment.

The experiences of your life and the way they shape your perceptions of food, along with your own intuition, are ultimately more important than any stated correspondence in any magical resource, no matter how trustworthy.

TABLES OF CORRESPONDENCE FOR THE KITCHEN WITCH

Here, you will find four tables of correspondence you may find useful. Remember, you should always trust your intuition when selecting ingredients. As you become more experienced, much of this will become second nature. For newer kitchen witches, though, these tables can be used as solid foundations in your new practice.

Pantry Staples and Magical Goals	
FOOD ITEM	**MAGICAL GOALS**
Beans	Luck, money, divination, decision-making
Bread	Abundance, health, security, kinship
Butter	Spirituality, peace, relationships
Cheese	Moon magic, joy, health, completion of goals
Eggs	Fertility, mysticism, Goddess magic
Honey	Health, happiness, love, lust, sex, purification, wisdom, stability
Milk	Love, spirituality, sustenance, motherhood
Rice	Money, fertility, protection, good luck
Salt	Protection, grounding, purification
Sugar	Love, affection, banishing gossip
Vinegar	Purification, protection, cleansing (white vinegar)

Magical Uses for Foods According to Color

COLOR	RED	ORANGE	YELLOW	GREEN
MAGICAL ATTRIBUTES	Passion, courage, strength, intense emotions	Energy, attraction, vitality, stimulation	Intellect, inspiration, imagination, knowledge	Abundance, growth, wealth, renewal, balance
USED IN MAGIC FOR	Love, physical energy, health, willpower	Adaptability to sudden changes, encouragement, power	Communication, confidence, divination, study	Prosperity, employment, fertility, health, good luck
FOOD EXAMPLES	Apples, tomatoes, peppers, cherries, strawberries	Squash, pumpkin, cantaloupe, carrots	Lemons, corn, golden beets, bananas	Avocados, peppers, kale, lettuce, chard, zucchini, broccoli

BLUE	VIOLET	WHITE	BLACK	BROWN	PINK
Peace, truth, wisdom, protection, patience	Spirituality, wisdom, devotion, peace, idealism	Peace, innocence, illumination, purity	Dignity, force, stability, protection	Endurance, solidity, grounding, strength	Affection, friendship, companionship, spiritual healing
Healing, psychic ability, harmony in the home, understanding	Divination, enhancing nurturing qualities, balancing sensitivity	Cleansing, clarity, establishing order, spiritual growth and understanding	Banishing and releasing negative energies, transformation, enlightenment	Balance, concentration, material gain, home, companion animals	Romance, spiritual awakening, partnerships, children's magic
Blueberries, blue corn, purple potatoes (turn blue when cooked)	Eggplant, purple carrots, purple cabbage, plums	Onions, mushrooms, white rice, yogurt, all milks	Black beans, blackberries, chia seeds, black rice	Lentils, brown rice, wheat, grains, dark chocolate	Beets, rhubarb, ginger (pickled), raspberries

The Elements in the Kitchen

ELEMENT	MAGICAL ENERGIES	TOOLS	FOOD EXAMPLES
EARTH	Stability, discipline, prosperity, abundance	Plates, spoons, baking pans, cutting board	Grains, flour, root vegetables, cheese, maple syrup, peanuts
AIR	Intellect, communication, imagination, harmony	Forks, knives, blender, oven fan	Honey, bamboo shoots, rice, bananas, dandelions, corn
FIRE	Passion, illumination, transformation, enthusiasm	Skillet, oven, oven burners, grill, toaster	Hot peppers, salsa, basil, radishes, sunflower seeds
WATER	Emotion, sensitivity intuition, empathy	Cups, bowls, pots, sink, dishwasher	All beverages, lemons, lettuce, cucumbers, plums
SPIRIT	All	All	All

Culinary Herbs	
HERB	**GENERAL MAGICAL USES**
Basil	Fosters loving vibrations, protection, wards off negativities in a home
Bay Leaf	Protection, purification, healing, strength, good fortune, money, and success
Cinnamon	Love, luck, prosperity, success, raises spiritual vibrations
Dandelion (FRESH LEAVES)	Divination, interaction with the spirit world, wishes, fulfillment
Nutmeg	Money, prosperity, good luck, protection
Oregano	Peace, deepening love relationships, releasing old relationships
Parsley	Protection, money, luck, lust, strength, vitality
Rosemary	Love and lust spells, promotes healthy rest
Sage	Longevity, wisdom, protection, dispels negative energy
Star Anise	Luck, spiritual connection, psychic and magical power
Thyme	Attracts loyalty, affection, psychic abilities

Versatile Magical Foods

When you work with natural, whole foods like fruits and vegetables, you often interact with them in multiple ways (washing, peeling, slicing, chopping, squeezing, separating edible parts from inedible parts, etc.) before you add them to the dish you're preparing. Many of these foods offer opportunities to work a little magic into the process of preparing them for cooking. Here are three examples of commonly used ingredients—bay leaves, onions, and lemons—that can provide an added boost of magic:

Bay Leaves

Many recipes for soups and sauces call for bay leaves, which are associated with protection, purification, healing, strength, good fortune, money, and success.

Witches commonly use bay leaves in wish magic, writing their wish on a bay leaf and burning, burying, or placing it under their pillow. When it comes to cooking, charging a bay leaf with the energy of your focused intention before adding it to the pot brings a little magic to the dish, even if the overall meal is just a "normal" weeknight dinner. The leaf infuses the liquid with its flavor as well as its inherent magical energy.

To take this technique a step further, you can charge the bay leaf and then rub a thin layer of olive oil across it with your forefinger. Then, with a chopstick or other clean, pointed tool, write a word or draw a symbol that represents your wish. Visualize your desired outcome as you drop the leaf into the pot. (Don't forget to remove it before you eat—whether or not you're using it magically.) →

Onions

Onions have potent medicinal and magical attributes. They are found in an enormous variety of savory dishes around the world and in several different types of spellwork. Onions may be cut and buried for love spells or banishings; some people add onion skins to incense for banishing as well as for attracting money.

The act of peeling an onion in a magical mindset can enhance any magical meal you're preparing. It's particularly good for magic related to healing, clearing obstacles, dispelling negative emotions, and doing away with any unwanted influences. The next time you're cooking with onions, try visualizing the peeling process as a means of releasing what's no longer needed in order to get to the core of what you're seeking.

Lemons

With their cheerful yellow rinds, lemons emanate undeniably positive and vibrant energy. Added to soups, stews, beverages, and much more, lemons —used for their juice and their zest—play many different culinary roles.

In magic, lemons are used for healing, longevity, purification, and spiritual awareness, among other goals. Using fresh-squeezed lemon juice in your recipes is well worth the effort and allows you to take advantage of the seeds and the peel for spellwork.

The act of squeezing lemons can also become a small ritual in and of itself. Imagine that the juice pouring forth from the fruit is akin to the unseen blessings of the Universe now coming into your life, as a result of the co-creation between Nature's processes and your own effort. Allow yourself to feel gratitude for what is already good in your life and the excitement of knowing there's more to come.

Part Four

EDIBLE MAGIC

THE MAGIC 7:
Recipes for Ultimate Spells

THE NUMBER SEVEN IS HIGHLY SIGNIFICANT IN many spiritual traditions around the world. In Western esoteric systems, seven is usually associated with wisdom, metaphysical abilities, and spiritual growth. Even in mainstream culture, seven is typically considered a "lucky" number.

These seven enchanting recipes maximize your magical potential by including as many foods as possible that resonate with your goal. If you're a beginning cook (or a beginning magician), try them out as they're written here first. As you become more practiced, you may decide to substitute certain ingredients to tailor a spell even more to your specific goal or to simply enhance your enjoyment of the dish. Whatever you do, always remember to charge your ingredients, visualize your goal, and enjoy yourself throughout the process!

Fortification Veggie Soup

Almost every main ingredient in this physically nutritional soup is magically associated with protection. Secondary associations of several ingredients include health, strength, and peace.

NOTE: The key to making delicious soups is in tasting your concoction as you add your seasonings. Doing so can also help you keep your focus on your magical goal!

Serves 4

- 2 tablespoons extra-virgin olive oil
- 1 medium onion, chopped
- 1 large leek, trimmed, quartered lengthwise, thinly sliced, and rinsed
- 3 cloves garlic, minced
- 1 tablespoon chopped fresh rosemary
- 2 medium carrots, peeled and sliced
- 8 ounces (227g) fingerling potatoes, chopped into ½-inch (1.25 cm) pieces

- 6 cups (1½ litres) water or low-sodium vegetable broth
- 1 bay leaf
- 1–3 teaspoons dried thyme, sage, oregano, and/or marjoram, to taste
- 3 packed cups (100 g) trimmed, cleaned, and chopped kale leaves
- 2 cups (480 g) cooked lentils
- ½–1 teaspoon lemon juice, red wine vinegar or apple cider vinegar
- Kosher salt and freshly ground black pepper, to taste

- Heat the oil in a stockpot over medium heat; add the onions, leek, and garlic, stir well, cover, and cook until softened, stirring frequently, 5 to 7 minutes. Add the rosemary, carrots, and potatoes and stir well; pour in the water or stock and bay leaf. Bring the mixture to a boil, reduce the heat to a simmer, cover, and cook for 10 minutes.

- Stir in your choice of dried herbs and kale and continue simmering until the kale is wilted and the vegetables are tender, 5 to 10 minutes.

- Add the lentils and lemon juice or vinegar; season with salt and pepper and serve.

Successful Sesame Salad Dressing

The bright, beaming energies of lemon and sesame come together in this easy dressing. Sesame's many magical associations include success and abundance, attracting new opportunities, and renewing hope. Lemon juice brings an uplifting, happy vibration to any recipe but is particularly powerful here due to its prominence.

NOTE: You may need up to 6 lemons to get 6 tablespoons of juice, depending on how ripe the lemons are, but the work of squeezing the juice yourself is absolutely worth it!

Makes about 1½ cups (355 ml)

⅔ cup (158 ml) tahini (sesame seed paste)

2 medium cloves garlic, finely minced or grated

6 tablespoons (90 ml) freshly squeezed lemon juice

½ teaspoon kosher salt

5 to 7 tablespoons (60 to 75 ml) water

- In a small bowl, whisk the tahini, garlic, lemon juice, and salt together until smooth. Slowly whisk in the water, a tablespoon at a time, until the dressing is thin enough to pour.

- Let the dressing stand for 20 minutes before using. Store in an airtight container in the refrigerator for up to 4 days.

Lucky Money Stir-fry

Many of the ingredients below are associated with money, including the peanuts and ginger as well as all of the green veggies. Be sure to have all of your prep work done in advance, as you'll need to be stirring constantly once you've heated the oil.

Serves 4 to 6

For the sauce:

2 tablespoons soy sauce

1 tablespoon rice vinegar

1 tablespoon honey

For the stir-fry:

1 tablespoon coconut oil

1 medium yellow onion, chopped

1 to 2 jalapeño or serrano peppers, or to taste, stemmed, seeded, and minced

1 cup chopped broccoli florets, about 8 ounces (227 g)

1 packed cup thinly sliced green cabbage, about 8 ounces (227 g)

1 large carrot, peeled and diced

1 packed cup sliced shiitake mushrooms, about 3 ounces (85 g)

1 small green bell pepper, diced

1 cup chopped snow peas, about 4 ounces (113 g)

1 cup roasted, shelled peanuts, about 4 ounces (113 g)

1 tablespoon minced garlic, about 3 cloves

1 tablespoon peeled and finely minced fresh ginger

Steamed rice, for serving

- To make the sauce, whisk together the soy, vinegar, and honey until combined; reserve.

- To prepare the stir-fry, heat the oil in a very large skillet or wok over high heat until smoking. (To test the heat, drop a piece of onion into it; if it sizzles, the pan is ready.) Add the onion and fry, stirring constantly, for 1 minute. Add the minced chili peppers, broccoli, cabbage, and carrot, and cook, stirring constantly, until softened, 3 to 4 minutes.

- Add the mushrooms, bell pepper, snow peas, and peanuts and cook, stirring, until vegetables are softened but still crisp-tender, 3 to 4 minutes.

- Add the garlic and ginger and cook, tossing together, until fragrant, 30 to 45 seconds.

- Pour the reserved sauce into the skillet and cook, tossing to coat, for 1 minute. Remove from heat and immediately serve over steamed rice.

Tropical Love Smoothie

Most fruits have love as one of their magical associations, so if you're not crazy about mango or pineapple, feel free to make substitutions. This sweet recipe makes roughly four servings, so just divide the quantities in two if you only want to share it with someone special.

Serves 4

- 2 medium bananas, peeled and sliced
- 2 cups (473 ml) coconut/almond milk blend
- 1½ cups frozen mango chunks, about 8 ounces (227 g)
- 1½ cups frozen pineapple chunks, about 8 ounces (227 g)
- 1 tablespoon pure maple syrup
- 1 teaspoon vanilla extract

- Put the bananas, milk, mango, pineapple, syrup, and vanilla into the jar of a blender or food processor. Pulse to roughly chop the ingredients; scrape down the sides of the blender with a spatula. Blend on high until completely smooth, 1 to 2 minutes.

- Divide among 4 tall glasses and serve.

Juicy Potion for Releasing Old Relationships

Sometimes it's hard to let go of energetic ties to someone we've cared about, even when we know it's for the best. Whether it's a past love, a friendship that has run its course, or another type of relationship, this tasty and very magical concoction will help you release whatever feelings you've been holding on to. For extra power, make and drink this juice during the final days of the lunar cycle, just before the New Moon.

Serves 4

2 large sprigs very leafy fresh basil, stems smashed with the side of a knife

2 cups water

1 (3-inch [7.5 cm]) piece fresh ginger, thinly sliced

¼ cup (59 ml) honey

teaspoon ground turmeric

2 cups (473 ml) fresh grapefruit juice

2 cups (473 ml) fresh orange juice

⅓ cup (79 ml) fresh lemon juice

- Put the basil, water, ginger, honey, and turmeric in a saucepan and bring to a boil over medium-high heat. Reduce the heat to a simmer and cook for 5 minutes. Remove from the heat and let stand until cool. Pour the syrup through a fine mesh strainer set over a pitcher. Using a rubber spatula, press on the solids to remove as much liquid as possible. Measure 1 cup of the syrup, reserving the remaining for sweetening teas or other beverages.

- In a large pitcher, stir together the measured syrup, grapefruit, orange, and lemon juices until combined. Refrigerate until ready to serve.

Thai Yellow Creativity Curry

Yellow is a powerful color for creativity magic, as it's associated with the Element of Air. This delicious vegetarian curry maximizes the energetic potential of yellow, setting you up for a vibrant flow of creative energy and ideas in the days and weeks to come.

Serves 6

- 2 tablespoons coconut or grapeseed oil
- 1 medium yellow onion, thinly sliced
- 2 cloves garlic, minced
- 1 teaspoon peeled and finely grated fresh ginger
- ½ teaspoon ground turmeric
- 1 tablespoon green curry paste
- 1 (14-ounce [400 ml]) can coconut milk
- 1 large yellow bell pepper, stemmed, seeded, and thinly sliced
- 1 medium yellow squash, about 8 ounces (227 g), stemmed, quartered lengthwise, and sliced
- 1 (8-ounce [227 g]) can bamboo shoots, drained

- 1 cup (170g) yellow cherry tomatoes, halved
- 1 cup snow peas, about 4 ounces (113 g), halved crosswise
- 8 ounces (227 g) extra-firm tofu, drained and cubed
- 1 teaspoon fish sauce, optional
- ¼ teaspoon red chili flakes, or to taste
- Kosher salt and freshly ground black pepper, to taste
- 15 large fresh basil leaves, stacked and very thinly sliced crosswise into ribbons
- Steamed rice, for serving (add turmeric to the cooking liquid for maximum yellow creativity energy)

- In a very large skillet, heat the oil over medium-high heat; add the onions and cook, stirring, until softened, about 5 minutes. Stir in the garlic and ginger and cook until fragrant, about 1 minute. Add the turmeric and curry paste and stir until the onions are well coated. Add the coconut milk and cook, stirring, until the mixture comes to a simmer.

- Reduce the heat to medium-low, add the bell pepper and simmer until softened, 3 to 4 minutes. Stir in the squash, bamboo shoots, tomatoes, and snow peas, return the liquid to a simmer, and cook until the peas are bright green and the tomatoes are beginning to break down, 4 to 5 minutes.

- Remove the pan from the heat; stir in the tofu, fish sauce, if using, and chili flakes. Cover and let stand for 5 minutes. Season the curry with salt and pepper, stir in the basil, and serve immediately over turmeric-steamed rice.

Sweet Potato–Sausage Fertility Frittata

An ideal magical meal for couples looking to conceive, this egg-based dish is packed with ingredients that support fertility and enhanced sexuality. Of course, you don't have to be planning a family in order to enjoy this Asian-flavored frittata, whether for breakfast, lunch, or dinner!

Serves 4 to 6

For the slaw:

- 1 teaspoon soy sauce
- 1 teaspoon rice vinegar
- ½ teaspoon toasted sesame oil
- ½ teaspoon peeled and finely grated fresh ginger
- ¼ small head Napa cabbage, about 4 ounces (113 g), cored and very thinly sliced

- 1 small carrot, peeled and grated on the large holes of a box grater
- ¼ cup cilantro leaves, coarsely chopped
- Kosher salt and freshly ground pepper, to taste

For the frittata:

- 1 tablespoon extra-virgin olive oil
- 2 links chicken-apple sausage, about 6 ounces (170 g), diced
- 1 medium sweet potato, about 8 ounces (227 g), peeled and cut into ½-inch (1.25 cm) cubes
- 1 small red bell pepper, stemmed, seeded, and finely diced

- 1 bunch scallions, sliced, white and green parts separated
- 8 large organic eggs
- ¼ cup chopped fresh cilantro
- 1 tablespoon soy sauce
- 1 tablespoon rice vinegar
- ½ teaspoon kosher salt
- Freshly ground black pepper, to taste
- Toasted sesame seeds, for serving

- To make the slaw: in a medium bowl, whisk the soy sauce, vinegar, sesame oil, and ginger together until combined. Add the cabbage, carrot, and cilantro leaves and toss to coat; season with salt and pepper and set aside.

- To make the frittata: preheat the oven to 375°F (190°C).

- Heat the oil in a 12-inch (30 cm) nonstick skillet over medium heat. Add the sausage and cook, stirring, until browned and crisp, 4 to 5 minutes; using a slotted spoon, transfer to a bowl. Add the sweet potatoes to the skillet, reduce the heat to medium-low, and cook, stirring often, until browned and tender when pierced with a knife, 8 to 10 minutes. Add the red pepper and scallion whites and cook, stirring often, for 2 to 3 minutes.

- Meanwhile, whisk the eggs, cilantro, soy sauce, vinegar, salt, and pepper together until combined. Stir the sausage into the vegetables in the skillet and spread the mixture into an even layer in the pan. Pour the whisked eggs evenly into the pan, scatter the scallion greens over the top, and cook, undisturbed on the heat, for 2 minutes. Transfer the pan to the oven and cook until the eggs are set, 16 to 18 minutes.

- Remove the frittata from the oven and let stand for 10 minutes; using a rubber spatula, slide the frittata onto a large cutting board and slice into 6 wedges. Serve with the slaw mounded on top of each slice or on the side and garnish with sesame seeds.

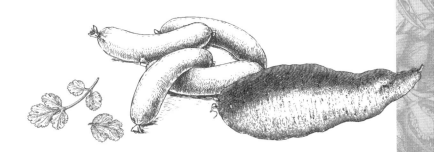

RECIPES FOR THE WHEEL OF THE YEAR

THE WHEEL OF THE YEAR PROVIDES A BEAUTIFUL framework for creating enchanted meals in tune with the seasons. It doesn't get more magical than working with the rhythms of the Earth's bounty. These recipes are perfect for a formal Sabbat feast or for enjoying during the weeks leading up to and following each holiday.

All Sabbat dates here correspond to the Northern Hemisphere. In the Southern Hemisphere, the Wheel of the Year is shifted in order to align with the opposite solar calander, so that Yule is celebrated in June, Imbolc in August, and so on. The dates for each solar Sabbat (the equinoxes and solstices) are given as a range, since the exact moment of each point in the solar cycle varies from year to year and across locations. For the cross-quarter Sabbats, which were traditionally celebrated from sunset to sunset, two consecutive dates are given.

YULE

(Winter Solstice) • December 20–23

Observed on the date of the Winter Solstice, Yule is considered the start of the new year in many Wiccan traditions. Rooted in the ancient pagan traditions of Germanic and Scandinavian cultures, this festival is both a celebration of the return of the waxing Sun and an acknowledgment of the coming winter. Magical themes include regeneration, setting intentions for the coming year, and nurturing your inner self.

~MENU~

LONG LIFE KALE SALAD WITH PEARS,
WALNUTS, AND LEMON VINAIGRETTE

WINTER SOLSTICE QUINOA WITH HERB-
ROASTED BUTTERNUT SQUASH AND PARSNIPS

YULETIDE CIDER-BRAISED PORK CHOPS WITH
STEWED APPLES, ONIONS, AND RED CABBAGE

RADIANT BROILED GRAPEFRUIT WITH
HONEY-NUT GREMOLATA

Long Life Kale Salad with Pears, Walnuts, and Lemon Vinaigrette

Pears are magically associated with longevity, lemon has purifying properties, and kale is known as a "superfood" for its many health benefits. This is a delicious dish to enjoy for a fresh start in the new year.

Serves 4 to 6

For the vinaigrette:

- 2 tablespoons fresh lemon juice
- 2 teaspoons Dijon mustard
- 2 teaspoons honey
- ¼ cup (59 ml) grapeseed or other neutral oil
- ½ teaspoon kosher salt, plus more to taste
- ¼ teaspoon freshly ground black pepper, plus more to taste
- 1 small shallot, very finely minced

For the salad:

- 1 bunch green kale, about 1 pound (454 g), tough stems removed, roughly chopped, rinsed, and dried
- 2 ripe Anjou pears, thinly sliced
- ½ cup (57 g) walnut halves, toasted and coarsely chopped
- 2 ounces (57 g) crumbled goat cheese

- In a small bowl, whisk the lemon juice, mustard, and honey together until combined. While whisking, slowly add the grapeseed oil until thick and emulsified; add the ½ teaspoon salt and ¼ teaspoon pepper and whisk well. Add the shallots to the dressing and whisk to submerge them.

- To assemble the salad, put the kale and half of the pears in a large bowl. Pour ¾ of the dressing over the greens, and using tongs, toss well to evenly coat; let stand 10 to 15 minutes (this can be done ahead of time and refrigerated; the dressing will soften the kale).

- To serve, season the dressed greens with salt and pepper and arrange them on a serving platter; drizzle the remaining dressing over it and scatter the remaining pears and walnuts over the top. Sprinkle the goat cheese evenly over the salad and serve.

Winter Solstice Quinoa with Herb-Roasted Butternut Squash and Parsnips

By the time of the Winter Solstice, the growing season for fresh produce has largely come to an end. But root vegetables like squash and parsnips, if stored properly, can still last well into wintertime, and when roasted and served with quinoa, they are simply divine!

Serves 4 to 6

12 ounces (340 g) butternut squash, cut into ½-inch (1.25 cm) cubes

3 medium parsnips, peeled, halved lengthwise, and cut into ½-inch (1.25 cm) chunks

Extra-virgin olive oil, as needed

1 teaspoon kosher salt, plus more to taste

¼ teaspoon freshly ground black pepper, plus more to taste

½ teaspoon ground cumin

½ teaspoon smoked paprika

1 teaspoon chopped fresh thyme leaves

1 cup (170 g) tri-colored quinoa, cooked according to package instructions

¼ cup (59 ml) sherry vinegar

2 teaspoons whole grain mustard

1 teaspoon Dijon mustard

½ cup (118 ml) extra-virgin olive oil

1 small bunch scallions, sliced, white and green parts separated

4 cups (120 g) baby spinach leaves

¼ cup (35 g) roasted, salted sunflower seeds, for garnish

- Preheat the oven to 400°F (204°C).

  - Put the squash and parsnip pieces on a baking sheet and drizzle some olive oil over them; toss well to coat. In a small bowl, stir together the 1 teaspoon salt, ¼ teaspoon pepper, cumin, paprika, and thyme until combined. Sprinkle the mixture over the vegetables on the pan and toss well to coat with the spices. Roast, stirring once, until golden brown on the edges and tender when pierced with a knife, about 15 minutes. Remove from the oven and cool on the pan.

- In a small bowl, whisk together the sherry vinegar, grainy mustard, and Dijon mustard until combined. While whisking, slowly add the ½ cup olive oil until thickened and emulsified; season to taste with salt and pepper.

- Put the scallions in a large bowl and put the hot quinoa and roasted squash and parsnips over them; let stand 10 minutes. Pour half of the dressing over the salad and toss well to evenly coat; season with salt and pepper.

- To serve, arrange the spinach leaves on a serving platter and mound the quinoa mixture on top. Garnish with the scallion greens and sunflower seeds and pass the remaining dressing at the table.

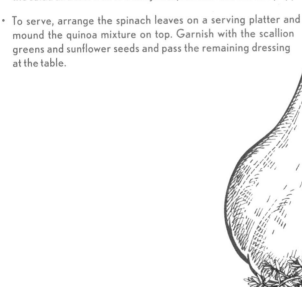

Yuletide Cider-Braised Pork Chops with Stewed Apples, Onions, and Red Cabbage

Cider is traditionally served at Yule celebrations. Here, it also flavors the heart of this deliciously seasonal dish.

Serves 4

4 bone-in thick-cut pork chops, about 1-inch (2.5 cm) thick (about 2¾ pounds [1.25 kg]), excess fat trimmed

½ cup (65 g) all-purpose flour

Kosher salt and freshly ground black pepper, as needed

3 tablespoons extra-virgin olive oil

1 medium yellow onion, sliced

3 cloves garlic, smashed

1 teaspoon fennel seeds

1½ cups (354 ml) hard cider

1 cup (236 ml) low-sodium chicken stock

2 sprigs fresh rosemary

2 crisp apples, such as Gala or Honeycrisp, cored and sliced ½-inch (1.25 cm) thick lengthwise and halved crosswise

½ small head red cabbage, about 1 pound (454 g), cored and very thinly sliced crosswise

1 tablespoon whole-grain mustard

Chopped fresh parsley, for garnishing

- Pat the pork chops dry with a paper towel and season them with salt and pepper. Pour the flour onto a plate and season generously with salt and pepper. Dredge the pork chops in the seasoned flour, tapping off the excess.

- Heat the oil in a very large skillet over medium-high heat until shimmering. Add the chops and sear, turning once, until golden brown on both sides, 3 to 4 minutes per side. Transfer to a plate.

- Add the onion, garlic, and fennel seeds to the pan, season with salt and pepper, and cook, tossing, until softened and beginning to brown, 3 to 4 minutes. Pour in the cider and stir, scraping up any browned bits in the pan. Add the chicken stock, rosemary, and apples, and bring the mixture to a boil. Push the apples to the outer edge and nestle the browned pork chops into the center. Return to a boil, reduce the heat to medium-low, cover, and cook, turning once, until the pork chops are cooked through and register 140°F (60°C) on a meat thermometer, about 10 minutes. Transfer the chops to a plate and cover tightly to keep warm.

- Raise the heat to medium high, stir in the cabbage, cover, and cook for 10 minutes. Remove the lid, stir in the mustard and continue cooking until the cabbage is soft and the liquid is thick and reduced by half, 5 to 6 minutes; season with salt and pepper.

- Serve the pork chops with the braised cabbage and apples alongside and garnish with parsley.

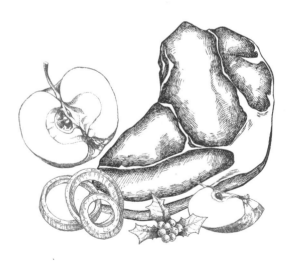

Radiant Broiled Grapefruit with Honey-Nut Gremolata

Celebrate the rebirth of the Sun God with this uniquely bright dessert.

Serves 4

3 tablespoons (28 g) walnut pieces

2 tablespoons (28 g) shelled pistachios

2 tablespoons (28 g) slivered almonds

1 teaspoon honey

1 tablespoon finely chopped fresh mint

2 ruby red grapefruit

3 tablespoons (36 g) light brown sugar

¼ teaspoon ground ginger

¼ teaspoon cinnamon

¼ teaspoon kosher salt

⅓ cup (80 g) fresh ricotta, for serving

- Position an oven rack 6 inches below the broiler and preheat the oven to 375°F (190°C).

- Spread the walnuts, pistachios, and almonds on a baking sheet and toast in the oven until light golden brown, about 4 minutes (be careful not to over-toast or the nuts will be bitter.) Remove the nuts and turn the broiler function on.

- Halve the grapefruit and slice a small piece off the center of the bottoms so they sit evenly upright and put them on a baking sheet. Using a small paring knife or grapefruit knife, cut the segments to loosen them from the membrane, leaving them intact. In a small bowl, stir together the brown sugar, ginger, cinnamon, and salt and evenly sprinkle it over the surface of the grapefruit flesh. Transfer to the oven and broil until bubbly, caramelized, and golden brown, 2 to 3 minutes.

- Meanwhile, finely chop the nuts and transfer them to a medium bowl. Add the honey and mint and stir to combine.

- To serve, put the broiled grapefruit on serving plates. Spoon a heaping tablespoon of the ricotta onto the center of each grapefruit; scatter ¼ of the gremolata over each grapefruit half and serve.

IMBOLC

February 1–2

For the ancient Celts, Imbolc marked the halfway point of the dark half of the year. This Sabbat is a celebration of the coming end of winter and the beginning of the new agricultural season. As you prepare your Imbolc feast, light a white candle to place on your kitchen window or on your altar to welcome the strengthening Sun.

~MENU~

ROASTED CAULIFLOWER AND
LEEK RENEWAL SOUP

BRIGHID'S MAC AND CHEESE
WITH GREENS AND LEEKS

SACRED SALMON WITH CELERIAC-TURNIP
MASH AND SCALLION BUTTER

PARSNIP—CREAM CHEESE
CENTERING CAKE

Roasted Cauliflower and Leek Renewal Soup

This refreshing soup signals the coming close of winter, as we eagerly anticipate the start of the lush growing seasons of spring, summer, and autumn.

Serves 6 to 8

1 head cauliflower, about 2½ pounds (1.25 kg), coarsely chopped

Extra-virgin olive oil, as needed

Kosher salt and freshly ground black pepper, to taste

1 large leek, trimmed and sliced, white and light green parts separated, rinsed

3 stalks celery, chopped

3 cloves garlic, coarsely chopped

2 quarts (2 l) low-sodium vegetable or chicken broth

½ teaspoon ground cumin

1 bay leaf

2 tablespoons red wine vinegar

Sliced chives, for garnish

- Preheat the oven to 425°F (218°C).

- Put the cauliflower on a baking sheet and toss with olive oil to coat. Season with salt and pepper and roast until beginning to brown, about 20 minutes.

- Meanwhile, heat 2 tablespoons olive oil in a large saucepan or stockpot over medium-high heat. Add the leek whites, celery, and garlic, season with salt and pepper, and cook, stirring, until softened, 6 to 8 minutes. Add the cumin and cook, stirring, until fragrant, about 30 seconds. Add the roasted cauliflower, bay leaf, and broth; bring to a boil, then reduce the heat to a simmer. Cover and cook until the cauliflower is falling apart, about 20 minutes.

- Stir in the leek greens and cook for 10 minutes, using a blender in batches, or with an immersion blender, puree the soup. Season with salt and pepper and stir in the vinegar.

- To serve, ladle into bowls, and garnish with a drizzle of olive oil and a healthy scattering of chives over the top.

Brighid's Mac and Cheese with Greens and Leeks

Dairy foods are sacred to Brighid, the ancient Irish goddess of fire, poetry, healing, and livestock (among other things), who is celebrated at Imbolc.

Serves 6 to 8

1 pound (454 g) cavatappi or fusilli pasta

10 tablespoons (140 g) unsalted butter, divided

1 large leek, trimmed and quartered lengthwise, thinly sliced, washed, and drained

½ cup (65 g) all-purpose flour

1½ teaspoons dried ground mustard

½ teaspoon sweet paprika

1 teaspoon kosher salt, plus more as needed

3 cups (710 ml) whole milk

8 ounces (227 g) sharp cheddar cheese, grated

⅓ cup finely grated Parmesan cheese

4 cups baby kale leaves, about 3 ounces (85 g)

¾ cup (57 g) panko-style breadcrumbs

• Preheat the oven to 375°F (190°C). Spray a 9 x 13-inch (23 x 33 cm) baking dish with cooking spray. Cook the pasta according to the package instructions, drain, and transfer to a large mixing bowl.

• Melt 1 tablespoon of the butter in a large saucepan over medium heat. Add the leek slices and cook, stirring, until softened, about 6 minutes. Transfer them to the bowl with the pasta. Add 8 tablespoons (1 stick) butter to the pan and heat until melted; add the flour and whisk until combined. Add the mustard, paprika, and salt and cook, whisking, until the mixture bubbles for a full minute. Slowly whisk in the milk, making sure there are no flour lumps remaining. Continue cooking, whisking frequently, until the mixture thickens and is bubbling around the edges, about 10 minutes.

- Remove the sauce from the heat and stir in the cheddar and Parmesan cheese. Let stand about 5 minutes. Meanwhile, melt the remaining tablespoon of butter and pour it over the panko in a small bowl; season with salt and stir to coat the crumbs in butter, and set aside.

- Whisk the cheese sauce until all of the cheese is melted and smooth. Pour the sauce over the cooked pasta and toss until well coated and completely mixed; fold the baby kale into the pasta and transfer the mixture to the baking dish.

- Sprinkle the buttered panko over the top and bake until the breadcrumbs are light golden brown and the sauce is bubbling, 15 to 18 minutes. Let stand 15 minutes before serving.

Sacred Salmon with Celeriac-Turnip Mash and Scallion Butter

In Irish mythology, the salmon is associated with wisdom, persistence, and strength. Many stories illustrate the benefits of connecting with the powers of this revered fish.

Serves 4

For the mash:

- 1 large celery root (celeriac), about 1½ pounds (680 g), peeled and chopped
- 1 large turnip, about 12 ounces (340 g), peeled and chopped
- ½ cup (118 ml) whole milk Greek yogurt
- 1 teaspoon kosher salt, plus more as needed
- Freshly ground black pepper, to taste

For the salmon:

- 1½ teaspoons smoked paprika
- ¾ teaspoon ground cumin
- ½ teaspoon kosher salt
- 4 center-cut skin-on salmon filets, 6-ounce (170 g) each, about 1 inch (2½ cm) thick
- 1 tablespoon extra-virgin olive oil
- 4 tablespoons (56 g) unsalted butter
- 1 bunch scallions, sliced, green and white parts separated

- Put the celery root and turnip into a medium saucepan and cover with water; add a large pinch of salt. Bring to a boil over medium-high heat, cover, and cook until tender and beginning to fall apart, about 20 minutes. Drain and return the vegetables to the saucepan. Add the yogurt, the 1 teaspoon salt, and some black pepper. Mash until broken down and chunky. Cover and keep warm while you cook the salmon.

- In a small bowl, stir together the paprika, cumin, and ½ teaspoon salt until combined. Sprinkle the spice mix evenly over the tops of the salmon filets; rub the spice mix into the flesh on three sides until absorbed. Heat the oil in a large nonstick skillet over medium heat until just beginning to smoke. Add the fish, flesh-side down, and cook, without disturbing, until the surface is golden brown and the fish releases itself from the pan, 3 to 4 minutes. Flip the fish, reduce the heat to medium-low, and continue cooking until just opaque in the center, 3 to 4 minutes more. Transfer the fish to a plate and cover to keep warm.

- Pour the excess oil out of the skillet and carefully wipe it clean with a paper towel. Add the butter and set the pan back over the heat. Cook, swirling the pan, until the butter begins to lightly brown and smells nutty, 1 to 2 minutes. Remove the pan from the heat, add the scallion whites and stir for 30 seconds; stir in the scallion greens; season lightly with salt and pepper.

- To serve, divide the celery root mash among 4 plates and top each with a salmon filet. Spoon the scallion butter over the top.

Parsnip–Cream Cheese Centering Cake

Parsnip, as a root vegetable, helps with grounding and centering in the midst of energetically intense times. It's also a wonderful late-winter alternative to carrots in baked goods. Try serving this yummy cake for "cakes and ale" at an Imbolc ritual or a Spring Esbat.

Serves 6 to 8

1 cup (130 g) unbleached all-purpose flour, plus more for pan

½ cup (56 g) whole-wheat flour

1 teaspoon baking powder

1 teaspoon baking soda

1 teaspoon ground cinnamon

½ teaspoon ground allspice

½ teaspoon kosher salt

1 stick (113 g) unsalted butter, room temperature, plus more for pan

2 ounces (57 g) cream cheese room temperature

1 tablespoon finely grated fresh ginger

½ cup (100 g) packed light brown sugar

3 large eggs, room temperature

1 teaspoon vanilla extract

⅓ cup (79 ml) whole milk, room temperature

1½ cups peeled and grated parsnips, about 2 medium, 6 ounces (170 g)

⅓ cup (35 g) chopped walnuts, optional

For the glaze:

½ cup (62 g) confectioners' sugar

¼ teaspoon ground cardamom

2½ teaspoons fresh orange juice

- Preheat the oven to 350°F (176°C). Butter and flour an 8½ x 4½-inch (22 x 11 cm) loaf pan.

- In a medium bowl, whisk together the flours, baking powder, baking soda, cinnamon, allspice, and salt until combined. In the bowl of a standing mixer fitted with the paddle attachment on medium-high speed, whip the butter and cream cheese together until combined, about 1 minute. Add the ginger and brown sugar and whip until lightened and fluffy, about 2 minutes. Reduce the speed to low and add the eggs, one at a time, scraping the bowl down between additions, until smooth; add the vanilla and mix well. Add the dry ingredients and milk in 3 additions, beginning and ending with the flour mixture.

- Remove the bowl from the mixer and, using a large rubber spatula, fold in the parsnips and walnuts, if using. Transfer the batter to the prepared pan and spread with the spatula into the corners of the pan. Bake in the center of the oven until set, golden brown, and a toothpick inserted in the center comes out clean, 45 to 50 minutes. Cool in the pan for 15 minutes before inverting onto a rack and cooling completely before glazing

- To make the glaze, whisk the confectioners' sugar, cardamom, and orange juice together until smooth. Using a spoon, glaze the top of the cooled cake, allowing it to drip down the sides. Let the cake stand until the glaze is set before slicing.

OSTARA

(Vernal Equinox) • March 20–23

Named for the ancient Germanic goddess Eostre, who is associated with spring and fertility, Ostara marks the Spring Equinox, or the halfway point between the Solstices. Night and day are of equal length on this Sabbat, making it a perfect time to meditate on the necessity of balance in our lives. Other magical themes include renewal, hope, beginnings, and new possibilities as we move into the warmer months of the year.

~MENU~

CREAMY RUTABAGA AND PARSNIP SPRING SOUP WITH PICKLED RADISHES

WISH-GRANTING DANDELION SALAD WITH EGGS AND BACON

WAXING LIGHT PASTA PRIMAVERA

EOSTRE'S HERB AND GARLIC GRILLED CHICKEN AND ASPARAGUS WITH BALSAMIC GLAZE

Creamy Rutabaga and Parsnip Spring Soup with Pickled Radishes

Rutabaga's magical energies are great for boosting self-confidence in social situations. Try serving this soup at an Ostara feast or bring it to a spring potluck—you'll enjoy yourself more and the others will love the soup!

Serves 4 to 6

2 tablespoons unsalted butter

1 medium yellow onion, chopped

2 stalks celery, diced

1½ pounds (680 g) rutabagas, peeled and chopped into small chunks

1 quart (1 l) low-sodium chicken broth

1 bay leaf

1 tablespoon chopped fresh sage

1 pound (454 g) parsnips (about 3 medium), peeled and chopped

2 cups (473 ml) whole milk

½ cup (115 g) whole-milk Greek yogurt

¼ teaspoon ground cumin

Pinch cayenne pepper, or to taste

Kosher salt and freshly ground black pepper, to taste

6 large red or purple radishes, cut into matchsticks

3 tablespoons rice vinegar

- Melt the butter in a large saucepan over medium heat. Add the onions and celery and cook, stirring, until softened, about 5 minutes. Add the rutabagas, chicken broth, bay leaf, and sage and bring to a boil. Reduce the heat to a simmer, cover, and cook for 30 minutes; add the parsnips and continue simmering until the vegetables are completely soft, about 20 minutes more. Remove the bay leaf and discard.

- Using a blender in batches, or with an immersion blender, puree the soup until smooth and return it to the pan over medium-low heat. Add the milk and cook until just beginning to simmer. Remove from the heat and whisk in the yogurt, cumin, and cayenne; season with salt and pepper and keep warm, without boiling, over very low heat until ready to serve.

- While the soup is cooking put the radishes in a glass bowl, sprinkle a little salt over them and add the vinegar, making sure the radishes are submerged. Let stand for 10 to 15 minutes; drain.

- Ladle the soup into bowls and gently rest a spoonful of the pickled radish on the center of the soup in each bowl and grind some fresh pepper over the top.

Wish-Granting Dandelion Salad with Eggs and Bacon

Not only is this a perfect spring recipe, but the magical properties of dandelion make it excellent for use in any spellwork related to granting wishes.

Serves 4

8 slices bacon

2 tablespoons balsamic vinegar

2 teaspoons Dijon mustard

2 tablespoons extra-virgin olive oil

Kosher salt and freshly ground black pepper to taste

1 teaspoon white vinegar

8 large eggs

1 bunch dandelion greens, about 8 ounces (227 g), trimmed, washed, and coarsely chopped

4 red radishes, very thinly sliced

1 cup (170 g) cooked and seasoned French green or brown lentils

- Cook the bacon in a large skillet over medium-low heat, turning once, until crisp, 10 to 12 minutes. Transfer the bacon to a paper towel–lined plate to drain. Measure 1 tablespoon of the bacon grease and put it in a small bowl; add the balsamic vinegar and mustard and whisk well. While whisking, slowly add the olive oil until emulsified and thick. Season with salt and pepper and set the dressing aside.

- Fill a deep skillet or saucepan with 3 inches of water and add the white vinegar. Bring to a simmer over medium heat; reduce the heat to maintain a gentle simmer. Crack the eggs, one at a time, into a small bowl and gently slip each egg into the hot water. (Make sure the water does not boil, but just has a few simmering bubbles rising in it or the yolks will break.)

Cook the eggs until the whites are completely set but yolks are still runny in the center, 4 to 5 minutes. Using a slotted spoon, transfer the eggs to a paper towel–lined plate to drain briefly.

- To assemble the salads, put the greens in a large bowl, add the radishes, and drizzle about 2 tablespoons of the dressing over them. Season with salt and pepper and toss well to coat. Divide the greens among 4 plates and scatter the lentils evenly over each. Rest two poached eggs in the center of each salad and crumble the bacon over the top. Serve immediately and pass the remaining dressing at the table.

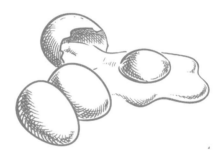

Waxing Light Pasta Primavera

Ostara is a time when the increasing strength of the Sun truly becomes apparent, after the brief moment of exact equality between night and day. Celebrate the waxing light with this energizing meal.

Serves 6 to 8

2 tablespoons kosher salt, plus more as needed

1 tablespoon extra-virgin olive oil, plus more as needed

1 pound (454 g) cremini mushrooms, sliced

Freshly ground black pepper, to taste

2 cloves garlic, grated

1 pound linguini or fettuccini, broken in half

2 large broccoli crowns, about 12 ounces (340 g), trimmed and cut into small florets

½ large bunch asparagus, 6–8 spears (about 8 ounces [227 g]), trimmed and thinly sliced on the diagonal

1 medium carrot, about 4 ounces (114 g), peeled and grated on the large holes of a box grater

4 tablespoons (56 g) unsalted butter

1 cup finely grated Parmesan cheese, plus more for serving

¼ cup chopped fresh basil

1 cup (170 g) grape or cherry tomatoes, halved

- Bring a large pot of water to a boil and add 2 tablespoons salt.

- Heat the 1 tablespoon oil in a large skillet over medium-high heat. Add the mushrooms, season with salt and pepper and cook, stirring, until browned and no longer releasing liquid, 6 to 8 minutes. Remove from the heat and stir in the garlic.

- When the water is boiling, add the pasta and cook according to the package instructions. Two minutes before the cooking time is up, carefully remove

1 cup of the cooking water and set aside. Add the broccoli and asparagus directly to the pot, stir, and continue cooking until the pasta is al dente. Just before draining, stir in the carrot and cook for about 30 seconds. Drain in a colander and return the pasta and veggies to the pot.

- Add the cooked mushrooms, butter, and ½ cup of the cooking water and toss well until the butter is melted and the pasta is coated and silky. Add the Parmesan and stir. Add more cooking water, if needed, and toss until the pasta is well moistened and saucy. Season to taste and stir in the basil.

  - Transfer the pasta to a serving platter and garnish with the tomatoes. Serve more Parmesan and olive oil for drizzling at the table.

Eostre's Herb and Garlic Grilled Chicken and Asparagus with Balsamic Glaze

Eostre is a Germanic goddess associated with springtime and fertility. It was likely from a festival in her honor that the Christian holiday Easter got its name.

Serves 4

¼ cup (59 ml) extra-virgin olive oil

2 tablespoons chopped fresh parsley, plus more for serving

1 tablespoon chopped fresh oregano

1 teaspoon chopped fresh thyme leaves

2 small garlic cloves, minced

Finely grated zest of 1 lemon

Kosher salt and freshly ground black pepper, to taste

4 boneless, skinless chicken breasts, about 6 ounces (170 g) each

1 pound (454 g) asparagus spears, trimmed

For the glaze:

½ cup (118 ml) balsamic vinegar

1 tablespoon packed light brown sugar

Pinch of salt

- In a large bowl, whisk together the olive oil, parsley, oregano, thyme, garlic, and lemon zest and generously season it with salt and pepper. Remove 2 tablespoons of the marinade and reserve. Add the chicken breasts, toss well to coat, and marinate for at least 30 minutes and up to 4 hours.

- Meanwhile in a small saucepan over medium-low heat, stir together the vinegar, brown sugar, and a pinch of salt. Bring to a simmer and cook until it's thick and syrupy and reduced by about three-fourths, about 10 minutes. Watch carefully and do not overcook or the vinegar can scorch. Cool to room temperature.

- Preheat a gas grill to medium-high or stovetop grill pan over medium-high heat. Toss the asparagus spears with the reserved marinade and season them with salt and pepper. Grill the chicken, turning once, until charred and cooked through (a thermometer inserted in the thickest part should read 165°F (74°C), 4 to 5 minutes per side. Transfer the chicken to a platter and cover to keep warm. Grill the asparagus, turning frequently, until charred and crisp-tender, 2 to 3 minutes total.

- Slice the chicken crosswise and serve with the asparagus alongside. Using a spoon, drizzle some balsamic syrup over them and garnish with parsley.

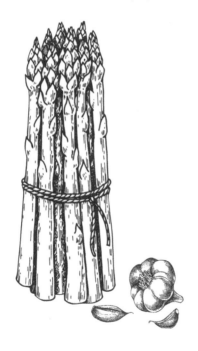

BELTANE
April 30–May 1

Beltane takes its name from the fire festival of the ancient Celts, for whom this day marked the official beginning of summer, or the light half of the year. A boisterous and merry time, Beltane is ideal for bonfires, beauty rituals, courtship, and lovemaking as the months of warm weather are officially getting underway.

~MENU~

ZUCCHINI AND GRUYÈRE HEALING
MAY DAY GRATIN

SEXY SPICED FARROW WITH RAINBOW
CHARD AND RADISHES

PSYCHIC SPINACH, MUSHROOM, AND
PROVOLONE STUFFED CHICKEN BREAST

FREYR'S STRAWBERRY-RHUBARB
CRUMBLE

Zucchini and Gruyère
Healing May Day Gratin

Beltane is a time to manifest vitality and wholeness. If you'd like some help getting the "spring" back in your step after a tumultuous time, put some extra magical energy into the shallots and thyme and visualize your goal as you stir them into the pan. Both are used in magic relating to healing from loss and trauma.

Serves 4 to 6

3 tablespoons extra-virgin olive oil

3 cloves garlic, very thinly sliced

3 large shallots, sliced

1½ teaspoons chopped fresh thyme leaves

Kosher salt and freshly ground black pepper, to taste

2 medium zucchini, about 1½ pounds (680 g), stemmed and sliced on the diagonal ¼-inch (6 mm) thick

4 ounces (113 g) Gruyère cheese, grated, about 1 cup

¼ cup (25g) finely grated Parmesan

¾ cup (58 g) panko-style bread crumbs

- Preheat the oven to 375°F (190°C). Grease a 2-quart (2 l) rectangular baking dish with cooking spray. Put the olive oil and garlic in a medium skillet over medium-low heat. Cook, stirring frequently, until the garlic sizzles and turns light golden brown (do not overcook or it will get bitter.) With a slotted spoon, transfer the garlic to a paper towel–lined plate to drain. Pour all but 1 tablespoon of the garlicky oil into a medium bowl.

- Return the pan to medium heat, add the shallots and thyme, and season lightly with salt and pepper. Cook, stirring, until the shallots are soft and beginning to brown, about 6 minutes. Remove from the heat and cool.

- To assemble the gratin, arrange the zucchini slices slightly overlapping in three rows in the bottom of the baking dish; season well with salt and pepper. Scatter the cooked shallots evenly over the top, followed by the Gruyère and Parmesan.

- Pour the panko into the bowl with the garlic oil and toss until the oil is absorbed. Season the crumbs with salt and scatter them evenly over the zucchini. Bake until the crumbs are golden brown, cheese is melted, and zucchini is tender when pierced with a knife, about 25 minutes.

- Scatter the toasted garlic slices over the top, if desired. Let stand for 10 minutes before serving.

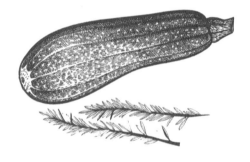

Sexy Spiced Farrow with Rainbow Chard and Radishes

Ramp up the romance of Beltane with radishes, which carry the Elemental energy of Fire and transform into sexual energy when taken into the body.

Serves 4 to 6

2 tablespoons extra-virgin olive oil

1 small sweet onion, diced

2 cloves garlic, minced

½ teaspoon ground cumin

½ teaspoon ground coriander

Pinch red pepper flakes

¾ teaspoon kosher salt, plus more to taste

Freshly ground black pepper, to taste

1 cup (200 g) pearled farro

2¼ cups (530 ml) low-sodium vegetable or chicken broth

1 large bunch rainbow, white, or red chard, about 1 pound (454 g), washed and sliced ¼ inch (6 mm) thick, stems and leaves separated

4 red radishes, thinly sliced

1 tablespoon (14 g) butter

3 tablespoons sliced or slivered almonds, toasted, for garnish, optional

- Heat the oil in a large saucepan over medium heat; add the onion and garlic and cook until softened, about 4 minutes. Add the cumin, coriander, chili flakes, ¾ teaspoon salt, and pepper, and cook, stirring, until fragrant, about 30 seconds. Add the farro and cook, stirring, until it begins to brown and smells nutty, 2 to 3 minutes. Stir in the broth and chard stems. Bring the mixture to a boil. Reduce the heat to a simmer, cover, and cook until the liquid had absorbed and the farrow is tender, about 30 minutes. Let stand off the heat for 10 minutes.

- Once the farro is cooked, melt the butter in a medium skillet over medium-high heat. Add the chard leaves and radishes, season with salt and pepper, and cook, tossing, until the chard leaves are slightly wilted but still crisp tender, and the mixture is hot, 3 to 4 minutes.

- Stir two-thirds of the chard and radishes into the farro and transfer it to a serving platter. Scatter the remaining chard over the top and garnish with toasted almonds, if using.

Psychic Spinach, Mushroom, and Provolone Stuffed Chicken Breast

Samhain is the Sabbat most known for being the time when the "veils" between the worlds are at their thinnest, but Beltane, which sits exactly across the Wheel from Samhain, is also such a time. Mushrooms are a powerful food for enhancing psychic awareness, making this an ideal Beltane entree.

Serves 4 to 6

- 1 tablespoon extra-virgin olive oil, plus more as needed
- 8 ounces (227 g) cremini mushrooms, stemmed and finely chopped
- 2 cloves garlic, minced
- Kosher salt and freshly ground black pepper, to taste
- 1 (5-ounce [142 g]) package baby spinach
- 4 slices provolone cheese, about 4 ounces (113 g), finely diced
- ¼ cup sundried tomatoes packed in oil, drained and finely diced
- 2 tablespoons pine nuts, toasted
- 4 boneless, skinless chicken breasts, about 2 pounds (907 g)
- Steamed white rice, for serving
- Paprika, for garnish

- Preheat the oven to 375°F (190°C). Line a baking sheet with aluminum foil and spray it with cooking spray.

- Heat the olive oil in a large skillet over medium-high heat. Add the mushrooms and garlic, season with salt and pepper, and cook, stirring, until the mushrooms are brown and have released all of their liquid, 6 to 8 minutes. Transfer to a bowl to cool. Add the spinach and cook, tossing, until wilted, about 1 minute. Season with salt and pepper and transfer to a colander to drain and cool.

- Squeeze the spinach to remove all excess moisture, roughly chop it, and add it to the mushrooms. Add the cheese, tomatoes, and pine nuts and toss well to combine. Taste and season with salt and pepper.

- Using a sharp knife, horizontally slice a thin pocket in one side of each chicken breast without cutting all the way through; open up the pockets and season the interior of each breast with salt and pepper. Stuff one-fourth of the mushroom mixture into each breast, close the pocket, and secure the filling inside with 2 toothpicks; transfer them to the prepared baking sheet. Brush the chicken with olive oil and season well with salt and pepper.

- Bake until the chicken is cooked through and a meat thermometer inserted into the center of the stuffing registers 160°F (71°C), 30 to 35 minutes. Cool for 10 minutes.

- To serve, remove the toothpicks from the chicken and slice crosswise about ½ inch (12 mm) thick. Arrange the slices over steamed rice and sprinkle paprika over them to garnish.

Freyr's Strawberry-Rhubarb Crumble

The Norse god Freyr, associated with strawberries as well as fertility, would definitely enjoy this dessert. The pairing of sweet strawberries and tangy rhubarb makes for a powerful romance-promoting recipe. Both ingredients are also associated with Venus, the love planet, and the Element of Water, where emotions reside.

Serves 4 to 6

For the crumble:

- ¾ cup (96 g) all-purpose flour
- ⅓ cup (30 g) rolled oats
- ¼ cup (50 g) packed light brown sugar
- 3 tablespoons sliced almonds
- ½ teaspoon ground cinnamon
- Pinch kosher salt
- 4 tablespoons (56 g) butter, melted

For the filling:

- 1 pound (454 g) strawberries, hulled and halved (quartered if large)
- 8 ounces (227 g) fresh rhubarb, sliced ¼ inch (6 mm) thick
- 1 teaspoon vanilla extract
- Finely grated zest of ½ lemon
- 3 tablespoons raw cane sugar
- 1 tablespoon cornstarch
- Vanilla ice cream or gelato or fresh whipped cream, for serving

- Preheat the oven to 375°F (190°C). Spray a 1½ quart (1.5 l) baking dish with cooking spray.

- To make the crumble topping: Stir the flour, oats, brown sugar, almonds, cinnamon, and salt together in a bowl. Pour the butter into the flour mixture and stir until coarse and crumbly and the butter is absorbed. Using your hands, squeeze the mixture into marble-sized clumps.

- Toss the strawberries, rhubarb, vanilla, and lemon zest together until mixed. Sprinkle the sugar and cornstarch over them and toss to coat. Transfer the fruit to the baking dish and scatter the crumble topping evenly over it. Bake until golden brown and the fruit is bubbling and hot, about 30 minutes. Let stand 10 minutes before serving with ice cream or whipped cream on the side.

LITHA

(Summer Solstice) · June 19–25

Also known as Midsummer and the Summer Solstice, Litha (an old Saxon word for this season) celebrates the ultimate power of the Sun as it reaches its highest point of the year. This is a highly auspicious time to gather magical, medicinal, and culinary herbs, and an ideal occasion for an enchanted picnic. Magical themes include abundance, growth, love, and masculine energies.

~MENU~

SUMMER LOVE CHILLED CHERRY SOUP
WITH FENNEL AND DILL

SOLSTICE WATERMELON SALAD WITH
CUCUMBER AND FETA

ABUNDANT ZUCCHINI AND SPICED
CHICKPEAS WITH BABY KALE

FIERY BLACKENED SHRIMP WITH TOASTED
ORZO AND SUMMER CORN PILAF

Summer Love Chilled Cherry Soup with Fennel and Dill

Cherries are often used in love spells. Seasoning this refreshing chilled soup with dill adds even more love energy to the recipe and is particularly useful for newlyweds who want their marital bliss to last a lifetime.

Serves 4

- 1 tablespoon grapeseed oil, plus more for serving
- ½ small sweet onion, finely chopped
- ½ small fennel bulb, about 8 ounces (227 g), tops trimmed, and fronds reserved
- 1 tablespoon honey
- 1¼ cups (295 ml) whole-milk Greek yogurt
- 2 cups (473 ml) unsweetened plain almond or soy milk

- 1 teaspoon kosher salt
- Freshly ground black pepper, to taste
- 1 pound (454 g) fresh cherries, pitted and coarsely chopped
- 2 tablespoons chopped fresh dill, plus more for garnish
- 2 tablespoons roasted, salted sunflower seeds

- Heat the grapeseed oil in a large skillet over medium heat until shimmering. Add the onion and cook, stirring, until softened about 5 minutes. Meanwhile, core the fennel bulb and finely chop it the same size as the onion. Add the fennel to the skillet and cook, stirring, until softened, 3 to 4 minutes. Stir in the honey until combined; transfer the onion mixture to a bowl and cool to room temperature.

- Whisk the yogurt and the milk into the onion mixture until well combined. Add the salt and a pinch of black pepper and combine. Fold in the cherries, cover, and refrigerate until cold, at least 1 hour and up to 4.

- To serve, stir the dill into the soup and ladle into bowls. Garnish each bowl with a sprinkling of dill, a drizzle of grapeseed oil, and some sunflower seeds and tear a few fennel fronds over the top.

Solstice Watermelon Salad with Cucumber and Feta

Watermelon and cucumber contain the energies of water and the Moon, and are both associated with healing. Bring this salad to a river, lake, or other body of water, and enjoy a peaceful, restorative picnic in nature.

Serves 4 to 6

6 cups (about 567 g) watermelon, cut into 1-inch (2.5 cm) cubes

½ English cucumber, quartered lengthwise and cut into ½-inch (1.25 cm) chunks

3 tablespoons fresh lime juice, plus wedges, for serving

1 tablespoon honey

1 teaspoon Dijon mustard

¼ cup (59 ml) extra-virgin olive oil

Kosher salt and freshly ground black pepper, to taste

3 ounces (85 g), about ¾ cup, crumbled feta cheese

Fresh mint leaves, about 8–10, roughly torn

• Put the melon cubes and cucumber in a large bowl and gently toss to combine. In a small bowl, whisk the lime juice, honey, and mustard together until combined; slowly whisk in the olive oil, and season to taste with salt and pepper.

• To serve, transfer the melon and cucumbers to a serving platter and drizzle 3 tablespoons of the dressing over them. Season lightly with salt and pepper. Scatter the feta and torn mint leaves over the salad and serve with lime wedges for squeezing over the top, and extra dressing on the side for passing at the table.

Abundant Zucchini and Spiced Chickpeas with Baby Kale

Zucchini is a go-to vegetable for any magical work involving abundance and fertility. Beans (chickpeas) and greens (kale) are also often eaten together to promote abundance.

Serves 4 to 6

1 teaspoon ground coriander

1 teaspoon ground cumin

½ teaspoon kosher salt, plus more as needed

¼ teaspoon freshly ground black pepper, plus more as needed

1 can (14½-ounce [411 g]) chickpeas, drained, rinsed, and patted dry with paper towels

2 teaspoons extra-virgin olive oil

½ small red onion, very thinly sliced

3 tablespoons rice vinegar

2 small zucchini, about 8 ounces (227 g) each, stemmed

5 ounces (142 g) baby kale greens or baby kale blend

½ cup (118 ml) Successful Sesame Salad Dressing (see page 121)

1 teaspoon toasted white sesame seeds

• Preheat the oven to 425°F (218°C). In a small bowl, stir the coriander, cumin, ½ teaspoon salt, and ¼ teaspoon pepper together until combined. Pour the chickpeas onto a small baking sheet and drizzle the olive oil over them; toss to coat well. Sprinkle the spice mixture over the chickpeas and stir well to evenly coat. Roast in the oven, shaking the pan a few times to prevent the chickpeas from sticking, until very dry and beginning to crisp and brown, about 15 minutes. Remove from the oven and cool to room temperature.

- Meanwhile, put the onion in a small bowl and toss with the vinegar and a pinch of salt; let stand about 10 minutes to soften. Using a vegetable peeler, peel long strips of each zucchini from end to end until you reach the seeds; flip and continue peeling until the just the center with the seeds is left; discard the cores. Cut the strips into roughly 2-inch (5 cm) pieces and transfer them to a bowl. Drain the onions and add them to the zucchini along with the kale greens. Drizzle about 2 tablespoons of the Successful Sesame Salad Dressing over the vegetables, season lightly with salt and pepper and toss well to coat.

- To assemble, arrange the dressed greens, zucchini, and onions on a serving platter and scatter the spiced chickpeas over them. Drizzle a little more dressing over the top and garnish with the sesame seeds. Serve immediately and pass the extra dressing at the table.

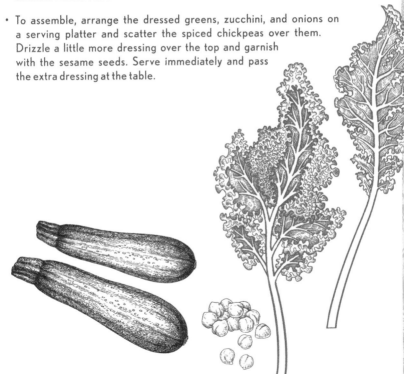

Fiery Blackened Shrimp with Toasted Orzo and Summer Corn Pilaf

This pilaf is packed with the summery energy of the Element of Fire, from the shrimp seasoning to the fresh corn.

Serves 4

1 pound (454 g) large shrimp (21–25 count), peeled and deveined

Extra-virgin olive oil, as needed

Finely grated zest of 1 lime, plus wedges for serving

1 teaspoon sweet paprika

½ teaspoon chili powder

½ teaspoon dried oregano

⅛ teaspoon cayenne pepper (add more for a spicier kick is desired)

1 small bunch scallions, sliced, white and green parts separated

1½ cups, 11 ounces (312 g) orzo pasta

3¼ cups (769 ml) low-sodium chicken or vegetable broth

½ teaspoon kosher salt, plus more to taste

Freshly ground black pepper, to taste

2 cobs fresh sweet corn, kernels cut from the cob, or 1 cup (6 ounces [170 g]) frozen corn kernels

3 tablespoons chopped fresh basil

· Put the shrimp in a medium bowl and drizzle 1 teaspoon olive oil over them; add the lime zest and toss to coat. In a small bowl, stir together the paprika, chili powder, oregano, and cayenne pepper and sprinkle the spice mixture over the shrimp. Toss to coat completely and set aside while you prepare the orzo.

· Heat 2 tablespoons olive oil in a medium saucepan over medium heat. Add the scallion whites and half of the greens and cook, stirring, until softened, about 2 minutes. Add the orzo and cook, stirring, until the pasta begins to turn golden brown, about 4 minutes. Add the chicken broth and ½ teaspoon salt and bring the mixture to a boil. Reduce the heat to a low simmer and cook, stirring frequently, until the orzo has absorbed the liquid, 16 to 18 minutes.

- Meanwhile, heat 1 tablespoon olive oil in a large skillet over high heat, swirling to coat the pan. Add the shrimp in a single layer and cook until beginning to brown and char, about 3 minutes. Flip the shrimp and continue cooking until browned and cooked through, about 2 minutes more. Transfer to a plate and cover to keep warm.

- When the orzo is cooked, stir in the corn kernels, remove from the heat, and cover the pan. Let stand about 5 minutes.

- To serve, taste and season the orzo with salt and pepper; stir in the basil. Divide the orzo among 4 plates and top each with cooked shrimp. Garnish with the remaining scallion greens.

LAMMAS/LUGHNASADH

July 31—August 1

Lammas takes its name from an Anglo-Saxon custom of blessing the first loaves of bread made from the first wheat harvest of the season. This Sabbat signals the coming end of summer and is the first of the three harvest festivals that will close out the Wiccan year. This is a time to appreciate the rewards of whatever our work has been over the spring and summer months, with respect to both the outer world and our inner growth.

~MENU~

FIRST HARVEST SUMMER SQUASH SOUP
WITH BASIL PISTOU

EGGPLANT AND MOZZARELLA
JUPITER NAPOLEONS

LUGH'S SPICE-RUBBED STEAK
AND SQUASH TACOS

LAMMAS BLUEBERRY-PEACH
MUFFINS

First Harvest Summer Squash Soup with Basil Pistou

Lammas is traditionally known as the "First Harvest," a time to celebrate the fruits of the labor of the growing season, while joyfully anticipating further harvests to come. Basil is a powerful herb for promoting love, fidelity, protection, money, and wealth.

Serves 4

For the soup:

- 2 tablespoons extra-virgin olive oil, plus more for serving
- 1 large sweet onion (such as Vidalia), chopped
- 2 cloves garlic, minced
- 2 bay leaves
- 3 stalks celery, sliced
- 2 tablespoons minced fresh oregano
- Basil stems from the pistou, below

- 6 cups (1.5 l) low-sodium vegetable broth
- Kosher salt and freshly ground black pepper, to taste
- Small pinch chili flakes, optional
- 2 small zucchini, 6 ounces each (170 g), stemmed, quartered lengthwise, and sliced ½ inch (1.25 cm) thick
- 2 small yellow squash, 6 ounces each (170 g), stemmed, quartered lengthwise, and sliced ½ inch (1.25 cm) thick

For the pistou:

- 1 cup (85 g) packed fresh basil leaves
- ¼ cup (22 g) packed fresh parsley leaves
- 1 small clove garlic

- Finely grated zest of 1 lemon
- ⅓ cup (79 ml) extra-virgin olive oil
- Shaved Parmesan cheese, for garnish, optional

- Heat the olive oil in a large saucepan over medium-high heat; add the onions and garlic and cook, stirring, until softened and just beginning to brown, 6 to 8 minutes. Add the bay leaves, celery, oregano, basil stems, and chili flakes; season with salt and pepper and stir until fragrant, about 1 minute. Pour in the vegetable broth and bring to a boil; reduce the heat to a simmer, cover, and cook for 10 minutes.

- Add the zucchini and yellow squash to the soup and cook until crisp-tender, 6 to 8 minutes. With a pair of tongs, remove the basil stems, squeezing them to release their juices into the soup. Taste and season with salt and pepper.

- While the soup is cooking, make the pistou: Put the basil, parsley, garlic, and lemon zest into a food processor and process until completely broken down, about 1 minute. Add a pinch of salt and the olive oil; puree until completely liquefied. Taste and season with additional salt and black pepper.

- To serve, ladle the soup into bowls and drizzle 1 to 2 tablespoons of the pistou over the top; garnish with shaved Parmesan, if desired.

Eggplant and Mozzarella Jupiter Napoleons

Eggplant is associated with the planetary energies of Jupiter, which can be used to promote prosperity, tolerance, and expansion.

Serves 4

- 1 cup (130 g) all-purpose flour
- ¼ cup (42 g) fine cornmeal
- 1 tablespoon kosher salt, plus more as needed
- 1 teaspoon freshly ground black pepper, plus more as needed
- 1 teaspoon dried oregano
- 3 large eggs, beaten
- 1 cup (70 g) panko breadcrumbs
- 1 tablespoon extra-virgin olive oil
- 1 medium globe eggplant, about 1¼ pounds (567 g), no wider than about 4 inches (10 cm) across at the widest point

- 1 cup (236 ml) Magical Marinara, or your favorite store-bought (see pages 89–90)
- 1 large ripe beefsteak tomato, about 12 ounces (340 g), very thinly sliced into 8 slices
- 8 large leaves fresh basil, plus more for serving
- 6 ounces (170 g) shredded mozzarella, preferably fresh
- ¾ cup (62 g) finely grated Parmesan cheese, divided, plus more for serving

- Preheat the oven to 425°F (218°C). Line two baking sheets with parchment paper

- Put the flour, corn meal, 1 tablespoon salt, 1 teaspoon black pepper, and oregano in a shallow pie plate and stir until combined. Put the eggs in a shallow, wide bowl; put panko on a large plate, drizzle the oil over it, and toss to evenly coat.

- Slice the eggplant crosswise into ¼-inch (6 mm) thick slices (you will need 12 slices). Working one slice at a time, press the eggplant into the flour mixture on both sides, shaking off the excess. Using a fork, dip the floured sliced in the egg, turning once and allowing the excess to drip off. Drop the coated eggplant into the panko, flip it once, pressing on it to adhere the crumbs. Transfer the breaded eggplant slice to the lined baking sheet. Repeat with the remaining eggplant and season well with salt and pepper. Bake until the eggplant is softened and panko is golden brown, about 20 minutes. Remove from the oven and cool briefly.

- To assemble the napoleons, place the 4 largest eggplant slices on one of the baking sheets. Spread 1 tablespoon marinara over each, followed by a tomato slice and a basil leaf. Evenly spread half of the shredded mozzarella over the four slices. Pick the 4 next largest eggplant slices and position them on top of the larger ones, pressing them lightly to compact the cheese and tomatoes. Repeat the layers of marinara, tomato slices, and basil leaves and top the stacks with the remaining mozzarella. Arrange the 4 remaining eggplant slices over the tops of each stack and spread 2 tablespoons marinara on each. Sprinkle 1 tablespoon Parmesan on each stack and transfer the pan to the oven.

- Bake until hot and bubbly and the cheese is melted, 12 to 15 minutes. Cool for 10 minutes before serving. To serve, garnish the stacks with fresh Parmesan, torn bits of basil, and serve warm marinara at the table for your guests.

Lugh's Spice-Rubbed Steak and Squash Tacos

Lugh is the Celtic god of craftsmanship and skill, and is also associated with the harvest and the Sun. In some Wiccan traditions, Lammas is known as Lughnasadh, the Celtic name for this feast.

Serves 4

For the tacos:

- 1½ tablespoons chili powder
- 2 teaspoons dark brown sugar
- 1 teaspoon ground cumin
- ¼ teaspoon ground cayenne pepper
- Kosher salt and freshly ground black pepper, as needed
- 1 pound (454 g) flank steak, trimmed and tenderized with a meat mallet

- 1 large yellow squash, about 12 ounces (340 g), stemmed, cut into thin 4-inch- (10 cm) long spears
- Extra-virgin olive oil, as needed
- Juice of ½ lime
- ⅓ cup (79 ml) sour cream
- 8 (6-inch [15 cm]) flour tortillas, toasted or grilled, for serving

For the mango-cucumber salsa:

- 1 ripe mango, peeled, pitted, and finely diced
- ¼ English cucumber, finely diced
- ½ small red onion, finely diced

- 1 small jalapeño, stemmed, seeded, and finely diced (use only half to reduce the spice level)
- ¼ cup chopped fresh cilantro
- Juice of ½ lime

- In a small bowl, stir together the chili powder, brown sugar, cumin, cayenne, 1 teaspoon salt, and ¼ teaspoon black pepper until combined. Remove 1 teaspoon of the spice mix and set it aside. Pat the steak dry with a paper towel and put it on a plate. Sprinkle the remaining spice mixture on both sides of the meat, rubbing it with your fingers to adhere. Let stand at least 15 minutes.

• Meanwhile, to make the salsa, stir the mango, cucumber, onion, jalapeños, and cilantro together in a bowl. Add the lime juice, season with salt and pepper, and drizzle a little olive oil over it to coat. Stir well and refrigerate.

• To make the tacos, heat a stovetop grill pan over medium-high heat until smoking, or preheat a gas grill to medium-high until hot. Put the steak on the pan or grill and cook without disturbing, until grill marks appear and the steak releases itself from the grill, 3 to 4 minutes. Turn the steak and continue grilling until desired doneness, about 3 to 4 minutes more for medium (140°F, 60°C.) Transfer to a plate and cover to keep warm. Sprinkle the remaining spice mixture evenly over the squash spears and grill them, turning once, until crisp-tender, 2 to 3 minutes.

• To assemble the tacos, stir the lime juice into the sour cream and season it lightly with salt. Thinly slice the steak against the grain. Divide the steak among the 8 tortillas, and top each with 2 or 3 squash spears. Fold the tacos in half and serve the mango salsa and lime cream for drizzling at the table.

Lammas Blueberry-Peach Muffins

Baked goods are traditional at Lammas, as this Sabbat marks the annual wheat harvest. Blueberries are used magically for protection, especially of children.

Makes 12

2 cups (260 g) all-purpose flour

1 teaspoon baking powder

1 teaspoon baking soda

½ teaspoon kosher salt

½ teaspoon ground cinnamon

¼ teaspoon ground nutmeg

½ cup (118 ml) low-fat buttermilk

½ cup raw (125 g) cane sugar

2 large eggs

¼ cup (59 ml) vegetable oil

1 teaspoon vanilla extract

Finely grated zest of 1 lemon

1 ripe peach, pitted and finely diced

½ cup (50 g) fresh blueberries

Demerara or raw cane sugar, for sprinkling

- Preheat the oven to 375°F (180°C). Line a 12-portion muffin tin with paper liners.

- In a large bowl, whisk the flour, baking powder, baking soda, salt, cinnamon, and nutmeg together until combined. In a small bowl, whisk the buttermilk, sugar, eggs, oil, vanilla, and lemon zest together until the sugar is dissolved. Pour the wet ingredients into the dry and stir gently with a rubber spatula until just combined; do not overmix. Add the peaches and blueberries and fold until the fruit is evenly mixed into the batter.

- Using an ice cream scoop, evenly divide the batter in the lined muffin tin. Sprinkle demerara or raw cane sugar over the tops of the muffins. Bake until golden brown and a toothpick inserted in the center comes out clean, 20 to 24 minutes. Cool in the pan for 10 minutes before transferring to a rack to cool completely.

MABON

(Autumnal Equinox) • September 20–23

With Mabon, the second of the three harvests, we return to the theme of balance, as the Autumn Equinox marks the moment of equality between darkness and light. Named for a figure from Welsh mythology, Mabon is a time to appreciate all that we have while also acknowledging that nothing stays the same for long, as soon the days will grow noticeably shorter. Magical themes for this Sabbat include gratitude, abundance, balance, and working with (rather than resisting) the flow of time.

~ MENU ~

ESCAROLE AND WALNUT PEACEFUL
CAESAR SALAD

ROASTED VEGETABLE AND BARLEY
BALANCING SALAD

AUTUMN POT ROAST WITH MAPLE
POTATO–BUTTERNUT PUREE

FRESH PUMPKIN PROSPERITY
PUDDING CAKES

Escarole and Walnut Peaceful Caesar Salad

Lettuces like escarole are associated with peace. Walnuts are helpful when undergoing transitions, such as the seasonal shift from light to dark that becomes more noticeable at Mabon.

Serves 4 to 6

- ½ cup (41 g) finely grated Parmesan, plus more for serving
- 2 tablespoons mayonnaise
- 2 tablespoons fresh lemon juice
- 2 teaspoons Worcestershire sauce
- 1 teaspoon Dijon mustard
- 1 teaspoon red wine vinegar
- ¼ cup (59 ml) extra-virgin olive oil

- 1 teaspoon kosher salt
- Freshly ground black pepper, to taste
- 2 heads escarole, about 8 ounces (227 g), trimmed, coarsely chopped, and washed
- ⅓ cup walnut pieces, about 1½ ounces (43 g), toasted
- Parmesan wedge, for serving

- In a small bowl, whisk the grated Parmesan, mayonnaise, lemon juice, Worcestershire, mustard, and vinegar together until combined. While whisking, slowly drizzle in the olive oil until emulsified and thick. Whisk in the salt and a good pinch of pepper.

- Put the escarole in a large bowl and drizzle half of the dressing over it. Add a small handful of grated Parmesan and toss well to coat the leaves with dressing. Transfer the salad to a serving platter and scatter the walnuts over the top. Using a vegetable peeler, shave strips of Parmesan over the top of the salad, garnish with more cracked pepper, and serve with additional dressing on the side.

Roasted Vegetable and Barley Balancing Salad

The balance between light and dark, and the knowledge that each season has its purpose, is celebrated here in this delightful and healthy dish.

Serves 4 to 6

3 cups (710 ml) low-sodium vegetable broth

2 cloves garlic, trimmed

1 cup (200 g) pearled barley

6 ounces (170 g) green beans, trimmed and cut into 1-inch (2.5 cm) pieces

2 large shallots, sliced

1 small yellow bell pepper, about 6 ounces (170 g), stemmed, seeded, and sliced into 1-inch (2.5 cm) pieces

1 small red bell pepper, about 6 ounces (170 g), stemmed, seeded, and sliced into 1-inch (2.5 cm) pieces

Extra-virgin olive oil, for roasting, plus ⅓ cup (79 ml)

Kosher salt and freshly ground black pepper, as needed

1 tablespoon white wine vinegar

2 teaspoons fresh lemon juice

1 teaspoon Dijon mustard

½ teaspoon honey

3 cups, about 3 ounces (85 g), baby arugula leaves

- Preheat the oven to 400°F (204°C).

- In a medium saucepan over medium-high heat, bring the vegetable broth and garlic cloves to a boil. Stir in the barley, reduce the heat to a simmer, cover, and cook until the barley is soft and liquid is absorbed, about 30 minutes. Remove from heat and let stand for 5 minutes to absorb any liquid still left in the pan.

- Meanwhile, put the green beans, shallots, and peppers on a baking sheet and drizzle with olive oil. Season with salt and pepper and toss well to coat. Transfer the pan to the oven and roast until veggies are browned, turning once, but still crisp tender, about 20 minutes.

- While the veggies roast, in a small bowl, whisk the vinegar, lemon juice, mustard, and honey together until combined. While whisking, slowly add the 1/3 cup olive oil until well blended. Season the dressing with salt and pepper.

- Remove the garlic cloves from the cooked barley and transfer them to the bowl of dressing. Using a fork, smash the cloves into the dressing until they are broken up; whisk the dressing well.

- To assemble the salad, put the warm barley and roasted veggies in a large bowl and drizzle the dressing over them; toss well to coat completely. Taste and season with salt and pepper; let stand 5 minutes for the dressing to absorb. Arrange 2½ cups of the arugula on a serving platter and mound the barley salad over the top. Scatter the remaining arugula over the barley and vegetables and serve immediately.

Autumn Pot Roast with Maple Potato-Butternut Puree

Perfect for sharing with a gathering of loved ones, this roast is packed with magical Earth energies. The golden potatoes and butternut squash in particular promote compassion and harmony among families.

Serves 4 to 6

- 1 (4 to 5-pound [1¾ to 2¼ kg]) beef chuck roast, excess fat trimmed, and tied
- Kosher salt and freshly ground black pepper, to taste
- 1 cup all-purpose flour
- 3 tablespoons extra-virgin olive oil
- 1 large yellow onion, chopped
- 6 cloves garlic, smashed
- 1 tablespoon tomato paste
- 3 medium carrots, peeled and chopped into ½-inch (1.25 cm) pieces
- 2 sprigs fresh rosemary

- 2 bay leaves
- 1 cup (236 ml) red wine
- 1 cup (236 ml) apple cider
- 2 cups (473 ml) low-sodium beef broth
- 1 pound (454 g) peeled, cubed butternut squash
- 2 pounds (907 g) Yukon gold potatoes, peeled and coarsely chopped
- 3 tablespoons (42 g) unsalted butter
- 2 tablespoons pure maple syrup
- 2 tablespoons red wine vinegar
- 2 tablespoons cornstarch
- Sliced fresh chives, for garnish, optional

- Preheat the oven to 325°F (160°C.)

- Pat the beef dry with paper towels and season generously with salt and pepper. Pour the flour onto a plate, season it with salt and pepper, and dredge the beef in it until coated on all sides, shaking off the excess. Heat the oil in a large Dutch oven over medium-high heat until smoking, Sear the beef until golden brown on all sides, 2 to 3 minutes per side. Transfer the meat to a plate.

- Add the onions and garlic to the pot and cook, stirring, until softened and beginning to brown, about 5 minutes. Stir in the tomato paste until combined; add the carrots and stir to coat. Season the vegetables with salt and pepper and cook, stirring, until the tomato paste begins to brown, 1 to 2 minutes. Add the red wine and stir, scraping up any browned bits in the pan. Cook until the wine is boiling and reduces by about half. Nestle the browned beef into the vegetables, add the cider, beef broth, rosemary sprigs, and bay leaves; bring the liquid to a boil. Cover the pot and transfer to the oven; cook until a knife inserted into the meat meets no resistance, 2 to 2½ hours.

- Meanwhile, put the squash and potatoes in a large saucepan and cover with water. Add a large pinch of salt and bring to a boil over medium-high heat. Cook until the squash and potatoes are beginning to fall apart, about 15 minutes. Drain and return the vegetables to the pot. Add the butter and maple syrup and mash until smooth. Season with salt; cover and keep warm until ready to serve.

- When the beef is tender, transfer it to a plate and cover to keep warm. Let the vegetables and liquid in the pot stand for about 10 minutes; use a large spoon to skim any excess fat from the surface and discard. Remove the rosemary and bay leaves, discard, and bring the liquid to a simmer over medium-low heat. In a small bowl, whisk the cornstarch with the vinegar until dissolved; pour into the simmering liquid and stir. Cook, stirring, until the sauce is thickened, about 3 minutes; taste and season with salt and pepper.

- To serve, slice the beef and serve alongside the squash/potato mash. Ladle the gravy and vegetables over the top and garnish with chives.

Fresh Pumpkin Prosperity Pudding Cakes

Pumpkin is used in food spells to promote prosperity and well-being. Squashes in general help to increase spiritual awareness.

Serves 6

- ¼ cup (50 g) organic white cane sugar, plus more for ramekins
- 1 cup (130 g) all-purpose flour
- 1 tablespoon unsweetened cocoa powder, plus more for serving
- 1 teaspoon baking soda
- 1 teaspoon pumpkin pie spice
- ¼ teaspoon kosher salt
- 1 cup (245 g) freshly roasted pumpkin puree
- 1 tablespoon molasses
- 1 large egg
- 1 teaspoon vanilla extract
- 6 tablespoons unsalted butter, melted, divided
- ⅓ cup mini chocolate chips
- 6 teaspoons light brown sugar
- ¼ cup (59 ml) hot water
- Sweetened whipped cream, or vanilla ice cream, for serving

- Preheat the oven to 350°F (176°C.) Spray six 8-ounce (118 ml) ramekins with cooking spray; sprinkle with sugar until coated, tapping out the excess. Put the ramekins on a baking tray.

- In a small bowl, whisk together the flour, cocoa, baking soda, pumpkin pie spice, and salt. In a medium bowl, whisk together the pumpkin, sugar, molasses, egg, vanilla, and half of the melted butter until combined. Add the flour mixture to the wet ingredients and fold with a large rubber spatula until just combined; add the chocolate chips and mix.

- Using a large ice cream scoop, divide the mixture among the prepared ramekins. Using a small spoon, smooth the surface of the batter in each ramekin. Sprinkle 1 teaspoon of the brown sugar over the top of each pudding. Whisk the remaining butter into the hot water, and pour about 4 teaspoons over the top of each pudding.

- Transfer to the oven and bake until risen and firm and the surface is beginning to crack, 25 to 30 minutes. A toothpick inserted into the center should come out clean.

- Let stand for about 10 minutes before serving with a dollop of whipped cream or vanilla ice cream and a sprinkle of cocoa powder on top.

SAMHAIN

(All Hallow's Eve) • October 31– November 1

Samhain is widely considered to be the ultimate Witch's Sabbat. Taking its name from the ancient Celtic fire festival which marked the end of the light half of the year and the start of winter, Samhain (which some scholars say means "summer's end") honors the "death" aspect of the life/death/rebirth cycle recognized by many Pagan cultures. This is the final harvest feast of the year and a time to have fun while preparing for the coming winter.

~MENU~

APPLE-POMEGRANATE DIVINATION SALAD WITH FETA AND PECANS

TRIPLE GODDESS SWEET POTATO, BRUSSELS SPROUTS, AND TOASTED GARLIC SOUP

"DUMB SUPPER" SAUSAGE AND RICE-STUFFED ACORN SQUASH

NATURE'S BEAUTY PASTA WITH GOLDEN BEETS, WALNUTS, AND GORGONZOLA

Apple-Pomegranate Divination Salad with Feta and Pecans

Apples were part of divination games and rituals during traditional Samhain festivities. Try your hand at a quick "yes-or-no" divination while preparing this salad. Ask a question and then slice an apple down the center. If the right half of the apple contains more visible seeds than the left, the answer is yes. If the left half has more seeds, the answer is no.

Serves 4

For the dressing:

- ¼ cup (59 ml) pomegranate juice
- 2 teaspoon Dijon mustard
- 1 teaspoon balsamic vinegar
- ½ cup (118 ml) extra-virgin olive oil
- ¼ teaspoon kosher salt, plus more to taste
- ¼ teaspoon freshly ground black pepper, plus more to taste

For the salad:

- 1 (5-ounce [142 g]) package baby arugula or mesclun greens mix
- 1 crisp apple, such as Gala or Honeycrisp, cored and thinly sliced
- ⅓ cup (42 g) chopped pecans, toasted
- 2 ounces (56 g) crumbled feta cheese
- ¼ cup (42 g) pomegranate seeds

- To make the dressing, in a small bowl, whisk together the pomegranate juice, mustard, and vinegar until combined. While whisking, slowly drizzle in the olive oil until thick and smooth; whisk in the salt and pepper.

- To assemble the salad, put the greens into a large mixing bowl and drizzle 3 tablespoons of the dressing over them; toss lightly to coat the leaves and transfer to a serving platter. Scatter the apple slices over the top of the greens and sprinkle with the pecans, feta, and pomegranate seeds.

- Serve immediately with the remaining dressing on the side, for drizzling at the table.

Triple Goddess Sweet Potato, Brussels Sprouts, and Toasted Garlic Soup

This hearty soup contains energies associated with all three aspects of the Triple Goddess—the Maiden (sweet potato), Mother (brussels sprouts), and Crone (toasted garlic).

Serves 4 to 6

- 3 tablespoons olive oil, plus more for serving
- 6 cloves garlic, very thinly sliced
- 1 medium yellow onion, finely diced
- 1 teaspoon smoked paprika
- ¾ teaspoon ground cumin
- ½ teaspoon ground cinnamon
- 1 teaspoon minced fresh thyme leaves
- Kosher salt and freshly ground black pepper, to taste

- 6 cups (1.5 l) low-sodium vegetable or chicken broth
- 1 large sweet potato, about 1 pound (454 g), peeled, and cut into ½-inch (1.25 cm) chunks
- 12 ounces (340 g), about 3 cups, fresh brussels sprouts, trimmed and quartered
- 2 tablespoons fresh lemon juice
- 2 tablespoons chopped fresh flat-leaf parsley
- Crisp croutons, for serving

- Put the olive oil and garlic in a large saucepan over medium-low heat. Cook, stirring often, until the garlic begins to sizzle and turns light golden brown, about 5 minutes. (Do not overcook the garlic or it will be bitter.) With a slotted spoon, transfer the garlic to a paper towel–lined plate to drain.

- Add the onions to the oil, raise the heat to medium-high and cook until the edges begin to brown, about 5 minutes. Add the smoked paprika, cumin, cinnamon, thyme leaves, and a hefty pinch of salt and pepper and cook until fragrant, about 1 minute. Add the broth and bring the mixture to a boil.

- Reduce the heat to medium and carefully add the sweet potatoes. Cook for 8 minutes; add the brussels sprouts and continue cooking until the potatoes are soft when pierced with a knife and the sprouts are crisp-tender but still bright green, 3 to 4 minutes more.

- Remove from the heat, stir in the lemon juice and parsley, and season with salt and pepper.

- To serve, ladle the soup into bowls, top with croutons and a drizzle of olive oil.

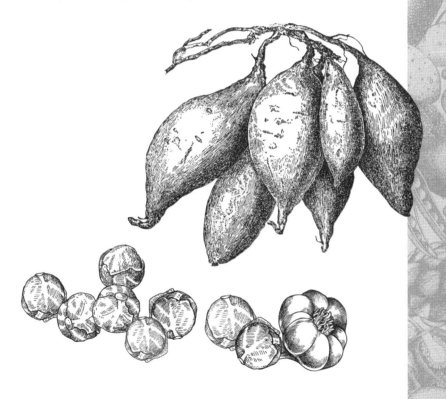

"Dumb Supper" Sausage and Rice-Stuffed Acorn Squash

The "dumb supper" is a Pagan Samhain tradition in which the ancestors and other beloved deceased family members are honored with a feast. A place is set at the table for the guest(s) from the spirit world, and the living eat their meals in silence in order to connect with the spirits of the departed. Acorn squash and sausage lend a traditional feel to this entree, perfect for your own version of the Samhain feast.

Serves 4

2 acorn squash, halved through the stem and seeded

Extra-virgin olive oil, as needed

Kosher salt and freshly ground black pepper, to taste

8 ounces (227 g) fresh sweet or spicy Italian sausage, casing removed

1 bunch scallions, sliced, white and green parts separated

2 cloves garlic, minced

8 ounces (227 g) cremini mushrooms, sliced

2 cups (300 g) cooked long-grain rice or wild rice blend

¼ cup roughly chopped fresh parsley, divided

1 tablespoon chopped fresh thyme leaves

⅓ cup, about 1½ ounces (42 g), shredded Parmesan cheese

2 large eggs, beaten

⅓ cup (79 ml) low-sodium chicken stock

- Preheat the oven to 375°F (190°C).

- Set the squash halves cut-side up on a baking sheet. Brush the interior of each half with olive oil and season well with salt and pepper. Roast until the flesh is tender when pierced with a fork, about 30 minutes. Remove from the oven and cool.

- Heat 1 tablespoon olive oil in a large skillet over medium heat. Add the sausage and cook, breaking up with a spoon into small crumbles, until browned and cooked through, about 5 minutes. With a slotted spoon, transfer the sausage to a paper towel–lined plate to drain. Pour all but 2 tablespoons of the oil in the skillet into a small bowl and discard. Add the scallions and garlic to the skillet and cook until softened, 1 to 2 minutes. Add the mushrooms, season with salt and pepper, and cook, stirring, until the mushrooms no longer release any liquid and are brown, 6 to 8 minutes. Transfer the vegetables to a medium bowl and cool.

- Add the cooked rice to the mushrooms along with the sausage, scallion greens, half the parsley, thyme, and shredded Parmesan and stir well to combine. Taste and season with salt and pepper. Whisk the eggs into the chicken stock, pour over the rice mixture, and stir until well combined. Fill each squash half with one-fourth of the stuffing and transfer them to the oven. Bake until very hot and the cheese is melted, 12 to 14 minutes.

- Let stand 10 minutes before garnishing with the remaining parsley and serving.

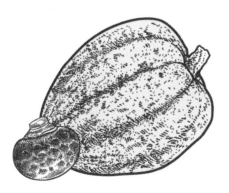

Nature's Beauty Pasta with Golden Beets, Walnuts, and Gorgonzola

Beets are magically associated with love, and in particular the love of beauty. As the brightly colored leaves fall from the trees, revealing the elegance of bare branches against the sky, this late-autumn meal reminds us to take in the unique beauty of each season.

Serves 4 to 6

- 1 pound (454 g) small golden beets, trimmed and scrubbed
- Extra-virgin olive oil, as needed
- 2 tablespoons kosher salt, plus more as needed
- 1 pound (454 g) orecchiette or penne pasta
- Freshly ground black pepper, to taste
- 2 tablespoons (28 g) unsalted butter
- 8 ounces (227 g) cremini mushrooms, quartered

- 2 cloves garlic, minced
- 1 teaspoon fennel seeds
- Pinch red chili flakes
- ½ small head, about 1 pound (454 g) Napa cabbage, cored and thinly sliced
- ⅓ cup (42 g) walnut pieces, toasted
- ¼ cup (20 g) finely grated Parmesan cheese
- 2 ounces (56 g) crumbled Gorgonzola

- Preheat the oven to 375°F (190°C). Put the beets on a large sheet of parchment paper, drizzle some olive oil over them, and wrap tightly in the parchment. Transfer to a baking sheet and roast until tender when pierced with a knife, 50 to 60 minutes. Cool for about 10 minutes, and then carefully rub off the peels with a paper towel. Cool to room temperature and cut into 1-inch (2.5 cm) chunks.

- Bring a large pot of water to a boil; add 2 tablespoons salt. Add the pasta and cook until just al dente, according to the package instructions. Remove 1 cup of the pasta water and reserve. Drain the pasta, return it to the pot, and stir in the butter until melted. Cover the pot to keep the pasta warm.

- Meanwhile, heat 2 tablespoons olive oil in a large skillet over medium-high heat. Add the mushrooms, garlic, and fennel seeds, season well with salt and pepper, and cook, stirring, until softened and browned, about 5 minutes. Add the cabbage and toss until just wilted, about 2 minutes. Pour the mushroom mixture over the pasta and put the pot over medium heat. Add about ½ cup of the pasta water, and heat, stirring, until simmering. Stir in the Parmesan and mix until the pasta is moistened and silky, adding a little more pasta water, if needed. Stir in the beets and cook until very hot. Add the walnuts and season with salt and pepper.

- Transfer the pasta to a serving platter and scatter the Gorgonzola over the top; serve immediately.

Afterword

COOKING AND MAGIC HAVE QUITE A LOT IN COMMON. Both involve the use of various ingredients and natural forces to create something new, and both are undertaken to improve the well-being of the practitioner. Most delightfully, both cooking and magic also present infinite possibilities—so much so that even the most experienced chefs and magicians can still learn new tricks, techniques, and ingredients no matter how many years they've been practicing.

Hopefully, you've learned enough from this book to inspire you to keep reading more about the endless ways in which you can combine the art of cooking with the art of magic. To get you on your way, you'll find a list of further resources to consult on pages 202.

As always, listen to your inner voice as you navigate new information. And remember to give yourself time to experiment with new recipes and techniques. You will learn much from both your successes and your mistakes (we all do make mistakes, after all).

May the magical energies of the Earth's infinite abundance be with you on your journey!

Acknowledgements

MY DEEPEST THANKS TO MY PARENTS, BROTHERS, aunts, uncles, and cousins for their eternal love and support. To Monica, Alex, and Sergio Haladyna for their enthusiasm, encouragement, and hospitality. And to Barbara Berger at Sterling for making this book a reality. Also at Sterling to cover art director Elizabeth Lindy for the beautiful cover design; interior art director Christine Heun; Sharon Jacobs for the stunning interior design conception, direction, and layout; production editor Ellina Litmanovich; and production manager Krista-Lise Endahl.

To my grandmother, who imbued all of her food with the magical energy of love, and who gave me the privilege of picking the cherries for her pies right from her own backyard. To Kim at Hedrick House, who literally had to teach me—at age twenty—how to chop a green pepper. (Not every kitchen Witch learns to cook from an early age!) To Dee at the Travelers Club International Restaurant and Tuba Museum, who taught me that intention and attitude are more important than exact measurements. And to Wesley Martin for his creativity and expertise in taking these recipes well beyond my humble culinary skills.

Suggestions for Further Reading

———◇———

Books concerning kitchen magic can take many different approaches. Some are cookbooks in their own right, consisting mostly of recipes, while others focus more on providing general information, tips, and kitchen-related spellwork. The resources listed below may fit either (or both) of these categories, but those with a heavy emphasis on recipes will be marked with an asterisk (*).

As with all things related to Wicca and Paganism, you may find conflicting information regarding magical correspondences, techniques, and other topics within these books. Think of these resources as jumping-off points toward your own exploration and discoveries in the realm of kitchen witchery—ultimately, experience will be your best teacher. Happy reading (and cooking)!

Scott Cunningham, *Cunningham's Encyclopedia of Wicca in the Kitchen* (Llewellyn, 1990).

Barbara Ann Daca, *One Pot Witchery-Stone Soup: The Hidden Grimoire of the Kitchen Hedge Witch* (CreateSpace, 2008)*

Anna Franklin, *The Hearth Witch's Compendium: Magical and Natural Living for Every Day* (Llewellyn, 2017)

Cerridwen Greenleaf, *The Book of Kitchen Witchery: Spells, Recipes, and Rituals for Magical Meals, an Enchanted Garden, and a Happy Home* (CICO, 2016)

Cait Johnson, *Witch in the Kitchen: Magical Cooking for All Seasons* (Destiny, 2001)*

Rachel Patterson, *Grimoire of a Kitchen Witch: An Essential Guide to Witchcraft* (Moon Books, 2013)

Shawn Robbins and Charity Bedell, *The Good Witch's Guide: A Modern-Day Wiccapedia of Magickal Ingredients and Spells* (Sterling, 2017)

Soraya, *The Kitchen Witch: A Year-Round Witch's Brew of Seasonal Recipes, Lotions and Potions for Every Pagan Festival* (Waverley, 2011)*

Patricia Telesco, *A Kitchen Witch's Cookbook* (Llewellyn, 1994)*

Leandra Witchwood, *Magick in the Kitchen: A Real-World Spiritual Guide for Manifesting the Kitchen Witch Within* (CreateSpace, 2015)

Jamie Wood and Tara Seefeldt, *The Wicca Cookbook: Recipes, Ritual, and Lore* (Celestial Arts, 2000)*

Index

Note: Page numbers in italics indicate recipes or rituals.
Page numbers in parentheses indicate intermittent references.

About the Author

---◆---

LISA CHAMBERLAIN is the successful author of more than twenty books on Wicca and magic, including *Wicca Book of Spells*, *Wicca for Beginners*, and *Wicca Herbal Magic*. Her Wiccan experience has evolved over years from a traditional practice to more eclectic explorations. Her focus is on positive magic that promotes self-empowerment for the good of the whole.

YOU CAN FIND OUT MORE AT: **wiccaliving.com**

Picture Credits

---◆---